Exposing Vulnerability
Self-Mediation in Scandinavian Films by Women

By Adriana Margareta Dancus

intellect Bristol, UK / Chicago, USA

First published in the UK in 2019 by
Intellect, The Mill, Parnall Road, Fishponds, Bristol, BS16 3JG, UK

First published in the USA in 2019 by
Intellect, The University of Chicago Press, 1427 E. 60th Street,
Chicago, IL 60637, USA

A catalogue record for this book is available from the British Library.

Copy-editor: MPS Technologies
Cover designer: Aleksandra Szumlas
Cover image: Painted by Khosrow Jamali
Production manager: Amy Rollason
Typesetting: Contentra Technologies

Print ISBN: 978-1-78320-988-0
ePDF ISBN: 978-1-78938-034-7
ePUB ISBN: 978-1-78938-033-0

Printed and bound by 4edge, UK.

This is a peer-reviewed publication.

Exposing Vulnerability

Contents

Preface

For several years now, I have been interested in the affective investments afforded by contemporary Nordic cinema, particularly Norwegian fiction film. As a Scandinavian scholar with an education background from Romania and the United States, I have been immediately drawn to grand, cathartic emotions like compassion, the love of nation, melancholia and nostalgia. Men, both in front and behind the camera, have populated my explorations, and concepts like masculinity and fatherhood have been central to my work. 2014 marked a shift in my research. I saw a film at the Bergen International Film Festival that shook me in ways that few other Norwegian films had done before: Solveig Melkeraaen's *Flink pike* (*Good Girl*), in which the director films her own struggle with severe depression. *Good Girl* troubled me and made me react viscerally, a response I also document in Chapter 1 of this book. During the public screening, I felt confused, vulnerable, even frustrated and wanted to exit the cinema hall as soon as possible. I am glad I did not. Instead I dwelled in that uncomfortable feeling which stayed with me long after I left the cinema hall, and which, at the time, I could not make much sense of. I started to work on an article about the film and dissect the 'ugly feelings' engendered by this film experience, to use a term coined by the American cultural theorist Sianne Ngai (2005). I also realized that Melkeraaen was only one of several other Nordic women filmmakers who stepped up in front of the camera in the 2000s to stage their own vulnerabilities for a larger audience. I watched these women's films again and again, in deep fascination, but also with dread. These films hit me in the gut and tested my limits (visceral, political, ethical). Film by film, one form of vulnerability after another, *Exposing Vulnerability* grew as a book.

The book project also came along at a time when my life took significant turns. After fifteen years of academic training in Scandinavian studies in Romania, Norway, Sweden and the United States, I got a permanent position as an Associate Professor at the University of Agder in Norway. Once again, I packed my things and moved from the Norwegian capital city of Oslo, where I was living at the time, to Kristiansand, a much smaller town situated 320 km southwest from Oslo. I left behind my friends and my now husband, boyfriend at the time, and committed to commute between the two places. This volatile living situation left aside, I loved my new job, the challenges and opportunities it provided.

Particularly in the beginning, I felt much more 'exposed' in Kristiansand. I will never forget the encounter I had with a little boy in the suburb where I first lived, and who, one day, ran after me eager for interaction. In dialect, he wondered where I worked, and when I answered I was teaching at the university, he put a sly smile on his face and said: 'You don't do that. I know you are a cleaning woman'. I said nothing, went inside the house and instantly burst into tears. It was not the comparison to a cleaning woman that upset me. To make ends meet as a student, I had taken cleaning jobs before. What bothered me was how deterministic and charged my Eastern European look became in the eyes of this little boy. While I brushed off this incident quite quickly, that feeling of vulnerable exposure has come back to me time and again while working on this book. Although I clearly realize that the women filmmakers' struggles documented in this book are certainly not mine, I am deeply grateful for the ways in which their films have given me the opportunity to work through my own vulnerabilities, as a woman in her late thirties, an only daughter (living abroad), a wife (working 320 km away from home) and a scholar interested in affect.

In my work with *Exposing Vulnerability*, I have received invaluable support. It is an impossible task to list everyone who has contributed to this project, yet I want to name those to whom I am most indebted. Anca Lungu, Elisabeth Oxfeldt, Julianne Yang, Per Thomas Andersen and Unni Langås read early drafts of the book proposal and provided constructive feedback that helped me frame the project. Gunnar Iversen was a close interlocutor during the last year of writing and read drafts of several chapters, for which I am deeply grateful. Thank you to Ralitsa Lazarova, who has read through versions of the manuscript and whose erudition and critical eye have strengthened my arguments and the legibility of this book. I want to express appreciation to my colleagues in the Research Group in Ethics and Trauma Fictions in Contemporary Culture at the University in Agder, who commented on various sections of this book. The film librarians from the National Library of Norway, Birgit Stenseth, Randi Østvold and Laila Johns, have helped me gather my corpus and obtain the necessary information from the film archives. I thank them for their support and enthusiasm for the project. I have also presented early versions of this work at conferences, annual meetings of professional organizations and seminars, including the Society for the Advancement of Scandinavian Studies, the European Network for Cinema and Media Studies, Sami Film Cultures organized by the National Library of Norway and the Centre for Norwegian Studies Abroad (SNU) at the University of Agder. At these venues, I have met known and unknown faces whose comments have been perceptive and have inspired me to continue my work.

I must also acknowledge my undergraduate and graduate students, who gave me the opportunity to test my ideas on a young generation for whom self-mediation is daily routine. MA student Mariell Johnson performed minute work when proofreading and formatting the reference and filmography lists as I prepared the manuscript for the peer review process. I also want to express my appreciation to Ph.D. student Bjørn David Dolmen from the Department of Popular Music at the University of Agder, who assisted me in decoding the music in the scenes from *Idas dagbok* (*Ida's Diary*) (Hanssen, 2014).

I am indebted to the National Library of Norway and Tore Dybing Myklebust, filmmakers Yvonne Thomassen and Ellen-Astri Lundby, production houses Medieoperatørene AS,

Fenris Film, French Quarter Film, Indie Film, Nordisk Film Production AB and Memento Film, who have kindly given their permission to use images from the films analysed in this book. Elin Johansen has helped me track down the origins of one of the archival clips used in *Min mors hemmelighet* (*Suddenly Sami*) (Lundby, 2009). Live Nermoen at the Norwegian Film Institute and Johan Fröberg from the Swedish Film Institute have promptly shared film statistics and helped me access information that was not readily available to the public. I have also received important institutional support from my home university. The Faculty of Humanities and Pedagogy at the University of Agder has provided generous funding for the publishing of the book. The BALANSE initiative has funded a much-needed research period that I used to structure my ideas and write the book proposal.

My close friends have contributed directly and indirectly to this project by stimulating conversations and engaging with vulnerability on so many levels, in so many forms, in inestimable nuances. I will not make a list of all of you. I trust you know who you are and how much I appreciate your friendship. Special thanks to Cecilie Endresen, whose generosity and brilliance has always inspired me to keep on delving into Nordicness despite trials, tribulations or insecurities. To Frida Andreasson, who has checked the accuracy of my translations from the Swedish films and read early versions of Chapter 6. And to Unni Straume, who time and again has provided insights from what it is like to work as a woman director in a male-dominated film sector.

Finally, *Exposing Vulnerability* is dedicated to my husband Øystein Sassebo Bryhni, whose love, wisdom and boundless patience have been essential in the realization of this book. When most things were in flux, I had you to hold onto, for which I am profoundly indebted.

Introduction

Women, vulnerability and first person filmmaking

In 2016, the Scandinavian term 'hygge' was adopted into the English language. In the British and World English Oxford Dictionary, hygge is defined as 'a quality of cosiness and comfortable conviviality that engenders a feeling of contentment or well-being' and is culturally tied to Denmark, although the concept is also very much a part of the other Scandinavian cultures (Oxford Dictionary). As several books on the English-speaking market advise, there are many ways to induce hygge, like lighting candles and/or a fire in a fireplace, indulging in freshly baked pastries or a freshly brewed cup of coffee, wearing soft wool and comfortable clothes, decorating interiors with woven textiles and sheepskin rugs, practising mindfulness, or enjoying intimate, relaxing moments with close family and best friends. In the bestseller *The Little Book of Hygge: The Danish Way to Live Well*, happiness expert Meik Wiking (2016) sees hygge as instrumental in explaining why the Danes are some of the happiest people in the world. And if Denmark topped the United Nations' World Happiness Report in 2013, 2014, and 2016, it was Norway that was ranked as the happiest country in the world in 2017 (Helliwell et al. 2017), while Finland reached a first place in the Happiness Report issued in 2018 (Helliwell et al. 2018). Like the Danes, the Norwegians and the Finns also know how to live the hygge way. In fact, Norwegians have the same word as the Danes, *hygge*, although it is most common to use the adjective form *hyggelig* rather than the noun, as it is the case in the Danish language.

If Scandinavians are eager to embrace hygge in their everyday lives (particularly in winter time when daylight in Scandinavia is limited and temperatures are low), it is striking how devoid of hygge contemporary Scandinavian cinema and TV are. On screen, Scandinavia feels dark and cold, unpleasant and harsh, disturbing and tormented, threatening and unsociable, depressed and discontent. In international successes like the Danish film *Jagten* (*The Hunt*) (Vinterberg, 2012) or the Swedish TV-series *Bron/Broen* (*The Bridge*) (2011–18), warmth, comfort and conviviality are strikingly absent. In Norway, the anti-hygge horror film has developed in spectacular ways in the 2000s. Low-budget Norwegian horror films like *Trolljegeren* (*The Trollhunter*) (Øvredal, 2010) and *Thale* (Nordaas, 2012) became international buzzes even before their release in Norway, while Norwegian directors of horror films like Tommy Wirkola and Roar Uthaug have successfully moved to making films in Hollywood. In Sweden, Ruben Östlund is a master of making the viewer uncomfortable by mocking political correctness and by depicting extremely awkward and embarrassing situations.

This cinematic anti-hygge has strengthened Scandinavia's reputation as an ambitious and innovative film region. In the 2010s, established Scandinavian male directors like Lars von Trier and Roy Andersson have continued to generate public and scholarly interest for their willingness to push aesthetical, political and ethical borders (Lindqvist 2016; Thomsen 2016). Scandinavian films in the grey zone between fiction and documentary like *Armadillo* (Pedersen, 2010), *Searching for Sugar Man* (Bendjelloul, 2012) and *Turist* (*Force Majeure*) (Östlund, 2014) have won prestigious film prizes. In 2010, *Armadillo* was awarded the Grand Prix de la Semaine de la Critique in Cannes, while *Searching for Sugar Man* received the Academy Award for Best Documentary Feature in 2012. In 2014, Ruben Östlund's *Force Majeure* won the Jury Prize in the Un Certain Regard section at Cannes, and in 2017, the director was awarded Cannes' Palme d'Or for *The Square*.

While Scandinavian male directors have received significant critical attention, Scandinavian women directors, who are equally bold in their readiness to test boundaries, have often been ignored by film scholarship. The Danish Susanne Bier and Lone Scherfig are among the few Scandinavian women directors who have generated more significant film scholarship (Hjort 2010; Molloy et al. 2018). Otherwise, it is still the case that film scholars are more likely to engage with the work of Scandinavian male directors while overseeing the contribution of Scandinavian women to film (Lian 2015). With this book, I want to correct this oblique scholarly focus by setting the limelight on the increasing number of Scandinavian films made by and featuring women filmmakers. These women step up in front of the camera to stage their own vulnerabilities with most pressing contemporary problems like mental illnesses, childhood and parenting in a digital age, bullying in schools, racism and the traumas of migration. There is not much hygge in these films. In fact, the films by and featuring women filmmakers commonly capture and produce a bestiary of affective responses such as frustration, confusion, contempt or disgust. Mixing and matching methods from documentary and fiction filmmaking, they blur the lines between life and art. They also challenge the international image of Scandinavia as one of the happiest and most egalitarian regions in the world by showing how real women (and their families) respond to and cope with contemporary problems like the ones mentioned above.

In my work in the archives, I have come across more than thirty Scandinavian films from the 2000s in which women filmmakers film themselves. This book draws attention to seven of them: *Flink pike* (*Good Girl*) (Melkeraaen, 2014), a film about the director's struggle with severe depression; *Brødre* (*Brothers*) (Holm, 2015), based on footage the director took of her two sons for almost a decade; *Återträffen* (*The Reunion*) (Odell, 2013), in which the director taps into her experiences with bullying in schools; *Idas dagbok* (*Ida's Diary*) (Hanssen, 2014), based on the video diary of a young Norwegian woman, Ida Storm, who films her fight against borderline personality disorder and self-harm; *Min mors hemmelighet* (*Suddenly Sami*) (Lundby, 2009) and *Familiebildet* (*My Family Portrait*) (Thomassen, 2013), where we see the directors attempting to recuperate a Sami identity that their families have denied them; and finally *Skörheten* (*Fragility*) (Bashi, 2016), in which the director investigates her panic attacks against a background of increased psychosocial stress and in relation to her family's migration history from Iran to Sweden. Later in this introductory chapter, I will explain why I have chosen to focus on these particular seven films. For now, let me underline that the films by and featuring Scandinavian women filmmakers do not come in negligible numbers in the 2000s. Nor do they lack in aesthetic quality, political boldness or ethical arguments.

Unlike other projects of self-mediation (e.g. blogs and reality TV), the films investigated in this book question the role of the viewers in consuming the vulnerability of others. Commonly shot over longer periods of time, they show that self-mediation requires massive affective and intellectual labour on the part of the filmmaker. For the Scandinavian women filmmakers do not just provide cameo appearances for fans to spot. Nor do they step up in front of the camera to temporarily ambush, as a male provocateur like Michael Moore would do in his documentary films. Instead, they expose their own embodied vulnerabilities in a wish to confront taboos.

Given the fact that film remains a bastion of male domination, it is noteworthy how women filmmakers from Scandinavia go about staging their own vulnerabilities to provide a diversity of perspectives absent from the anti-hygge male productions and other mainstream cinema. Particularly striking is how these women tap into their own experiences to engage with the politics of shame as a result of mental illness (e.g. depression, anxiety, panic, borderline and self-harm), loss (e.g. loss of children, parents or close family members) and discrimination (e.g. the histories of abuse against the Sami minority). It is this diversity of perspectives that this book seeks to unpack by analysing how Scandinavian women filmmakers make provoking films that matter.

Inspired by the work of affect theorists like Lauren Berlant (2011) and Sara Ahmed (2004a, 2004b), the book tracks down how the real, concrete affects staged in the seven films I have chosen, resonate across many different contexts (cultural, political, ethical, local, national, regional and global). The book also shows how Scandinavians construct meaning in their lives in an age of accelerated mediation, migration and terror, and highlights how the insights provided by the films analysed in this book speak not only of Scandinavia's exceptionality and uniqueness, but also of its interconnectedness with the world.

In this introduction, I start with a discussion of my corpus through the notions of women's cinema, vulnerability and first person film, three theoretical terms that must be addressed in a book about women filmmakers who make films about their own vulnerabilities. This will allow me to make explicit the scholarship on which this book builds as well as its contribution to film, gender and cultural studies. In addition to providing a theoretical framework to the book, the introduction also provides a brief overview of the chapters in the book and lists the analytical questions guiding this project.

Women's cinema: Scandinavian women in film

In *Women's Cinema, World Cinema: Projecting Contemporary Feminisms*, American film scholar Patricia White shows how a new generation of women directors from around the world are actively shaping the formations of world cinema through their participation in international film festivals and alternative cinema circuits, and by accessing transnational financing, digital streaming and online DVD-outlets. As White explains, although these women filmmakers reap the benefits of transnational feminist influence and activism, they do not necessarily identify themselves with a feminist agenda (2015: 18). White further argues that the films made by this new generation of filmmakers are 'worldlier than other types of films', although they travel outside national boundaries on the passport 'female director' (2015: 169). They intertwine the personal and the global, the national and the international, and in the process, they redefine both women's and world cinema.

Films made by and featuring Scandinavian women filmmakers in the 2000s are illustrative of the worldliness of the new women's cinema as discussed by White. As I will point out in each chapter, these Scandinavian films reach transnational audiences through international film festivals and digital streaming in addition to being broadcast on national TV channels. On the one hand, these films are personal and local, with the Scandinavian women filmmakers tapping into their own embodied experiences with depression, anxiety, panic, parenting, bullying, indigenousness and migration. On the other hand, the topics discussed in these films are of huge relevance to more than just women and more than just Scandinavians. The films show how the women filmmakers make sense of their lives in tune with the world, and not in isolation from it. Their struggles and dilemmas are not simply idiosyncratic. They use their own bodies to guarantee the authenticity of experiences staged in front of the camera and advance social claims that are not necessarily tied to a feminist political agenda of equal rights between men and women.

In her book, White is particularly interested in the articulation of gender, geopolitics and cinema. In that respect, she analyses feature films made by women directors from Argentina, Bosnia and Herzegovina, Canada, France, India, Indonesia, Iran, Lebanon, Pakistan, Peru, South Korea and Taiwan. She also briefly mentions Scandinavian women directors like Denmark's 2011 Academy Winner for Best Foreign Language Film, Susanne Bier. However, White's book does not provide any in-depth analysis of films by Scandinavian women filmmakers. Given White's preoccupation for the institutional shapes of film cultures, this neglect is in many respects surprising. Since the 2000s, Scandinavian film sectors have not only become globally orientated (Hjort 2005), but also gender-minded in ways that other national and international film bodies have not. This makes Scandinavian film a particularly interesting case to discuss women's cinema as world cinema.

As White also notes, gender imbalance is rampant in film. Around the world, women in key positions behind the camera are in clear minority. This is particularly evident if one looks at the very low percentage of women who direct big budget films. The most recent statistics show that women directed 11 per cent of the 250 top grossing films in 2017 (Lauzen 2018: 1). The pay gap between the world's top male and female actors remains significant despite recent efforts made by individual actresses in Hollywood to push back against the wage gap (Desta 2018). Only one woman has ever won an Academy Award for Best Director (Kathryn Bigelow for *The Hurt Locker* in 2008), and the same is true for Cannes' Palme d'Or (Jane Campion for *The Piano* in 1993). In addition, the #MeToo movement revealed how sexual assault and harassment towards women were problems that the film industry had silenced and dismissed for years.

The gender imbalance also manifests itself in the perspectives presented on the screen. To highlight the gender bias in films, Sweden has introduced a new rating system based on the Bechdel-Wallace test and which measures the active presence of women on screen (Associated Press in Stockholm 2013). For a film to get an A-rating in the Bechdel-Wallace test, it must feature at least two named female characters that talk to each other about something other than a man (Associated Press in Stockholm 2013). While the parameters used by the Bechdel-Wallace test are to be methodologically debated, it is nevertheless striking to see how often women on screen are presented as a nameless mass solely defined through their romantic relationships to men.

If major actors like Hollywood and the Cannes Film Festival have only recently started to discuss gender equality following public outcry and pressure from movements like #MeToo and Time's Up (Hutchinson 2018), small film nations like Norway and Sweden have for several years now addressed the precarious situation of women in film. In the second half of the 2000s, both Norway and Sweden committed to address gender imbalance on a political and institutional level, an unprecedented move that caught the attention of the international community. For example, inspired by Sweden, in 2016, the British Film Institute (BFI) declared their interest in following suit (Roxborough 2016). This speaks of the impact small Scandinavian film nations can have on the international arena and illustrates why Scandinavian film sectors deserve attention from scholars interested in the articulation of gender, geopolitics and cinema. I therefore want to address White's neglect and turn attention to the institutional shapes of Scandinavian film cultures from the perspective of gender.

I choose to focus on film examples from Norway and Sweden because these two Scandinavian nations have made gender equality into an important flagship of their film sectors. I also want to expand White's notion of women's cinema as world cinema by discussing film examples that do not comfortably fit the category of feature film. I will come back to the question of genre later in this chapter when I discuss the umbrella term 'first person cinema'. For now, let us look at the institutional context out of which the Norwegian and Swedish films analysed in this book emerge.

In 2007, the Norwegian Parliament issued a white paper on film policy that stated that women should account for at least 40 per cent of the key production staff in a film (Norway 2006–07). As the Norwegian government's civil executive body for the film sector and its advisor in questions of film policy, the state-funded Norsk filminstitutt (Norwegian Film Institute [NFI]) was given the mandate to follow up on this political goal in close collaboration with the film sector and film schools in Norway. In fact, the NFI set an even more ambitious goal for itself: half of the key production staff in a Norwegian film should be women by 2020 (NFI 2018: 26). One of the main measures taken so far by the NFI has been to practice moderate gender quotas in film projects pre-funded by the NFI film commissioners. In 2017, there were seven film commissioners at the NFI, each of them selecting a limited number of artistically ambitious projects to receive NFI-funding. The same year, the total funding granted by the NFI to development, production and promotion of feature length films, documentaries, short films and interactive games was 432 million Norwegian kroner (NOK) (NFI 2018: 19). Of this amount, film commissioners allocated 201 million NOK in grants for development, production and script development, which accounts for a little under half of the total funding available at the NFI (NFI 2018: 30). By moderate gender quotas, NFI means that projects with women in key production staff (defined as director, producer, screenwriter) are given priority when the film commissioner must choose from several equally rated projects (NFI 2017: 20). As noted in several yearly reports issued by the NFI, this measure is efficient when women represent a critical mass in the total number of applicants.

Another thing that the NFI does is to keep detailed statistics of women in Norwegian film. Counting women in film can be both depressing and relative, which may explain why scholars like White are weary of numbers. It depends what one counts and how one does it, and numbers by themselves do not give the entire picture, as White's research so well demonstrates. Some films simply fall outside the official statistics because they travel through alternative cinema circuits and/or digital streaming, which film bodies like the NFI do not keep track of. On the other hand, statistics are quite important in the Norwegian context because they help the NFI assess their work with the gender equality mandate that the Norwegian government has given them. In the annual report from 2017, the NFI uses three main criteria to measure the proportion of women in Norwegian film: (1) the percentage of female main characters in films released in a year; (2) the percentage of women directors, producers and screenwriters in films released in that year; (3) the percentage of women directors, producers and screenwriters in feature length, short and documentary films that received NFI pre-grants through the production scheme (NFI 2018: 27).

2016 is the first time NFI collected statistics on female main characters. In the annual report from 2016, there is no explanation about what NFI means by 'main character'. Yet, a report on the same topic commissioned by NFI in 2015 defines 'main character' as the character through whose eyes the viewers experience the story (Bjerkeland and Servoll 2015: 3). This suggests that the NFI used the same definition in collecting statistics. Of the 27 films released in 2017, six films had only women as main characters, three films had both men and women as main characters, while the remaining eighteen films had only men as main characters (NFI 2018: 28). The female shares of key staff in all films released in 2017 were 30.8 per cent (NFI 2018: 29). The percentage of female key staff in films that received pre-grants through the production scheme was 33.6 per cent for feature films, 35.0 per cent for documentaries and 55.6 per cent for short films (NFI 2018: 29). Overall, statistics show that 2014 and 2015 were record years for gender parity in Norwegian film (see Table 1 and 2). 2014, for example, registered the highest ever female shares for feature-length fiction films (53.9 per cent) and short films (61.3 per cent) that were granted funding through the production scheme (NFI 2018: 29). In the following years, these numbers decreased, which suggests that is is hard to sustain gender parity in film over time.

In order to achieve enduring effects, in 2016, the NFI developed an action plan that built on the work done in the past, but also announced active involvement in talent development for young girls and women, the introduction of moderate gender quotas in support schemes

Table 1: The female shares of key staff in all films released in Norway during the period 2011–17.

2011	2012	2013	2014	2015	2016	2017
25%	26%	27.7%	30%	34.3%	33.3%	30.8%

Table 2: The female shares of key staff in Norwegian films that received pre-grants through the production scheme at the NFI in the period 2011–17.

	2011	2012	2013	2014	2015	2016	2017
Feature films	31%	33%	38.5%	53.9%	35.7%	31.7%	33.6%
Documentaries	32%	41%	48.9%	36.4%	37%	53.9%	35.0%
Short films	42%	36%	44.6%	61.3%	50%	43.4%	55.6%

other than the artistically rated projects funded by the film commissioners, and a yearly report on gender equality in Norwegian film (NFI 2016). The last two actions were already implemented, starting with 2017 (NFI 2018).

Sweden, more so than Norway, has generated a lot of international interest for the way in which Svenska Filminstitutet (Swedish Film Institute [SFI]) has worked to achieve gender equality in Swedish film. Just like the NFI, the SFI is organized under the auspices of the Ministry of Culture. Its mandate is to preserve and promote Swedish film nationally and internationally through the allocation of state funds for production, distribution and public showing, among others. Like the NFI, the SFI also uses a consultant scheme whereby film commissioners share a significant part of the SFI's annual budget to support artistically ambitious projects. In the press, the person commonly credited for the gender revolution at the SFI is Anna Serner. After her appointment as the CEO of the SFI in 2011, Serner publicly summoned women filmmakers to apply for funding (Lange 2016). She also encouraged her film commissioners to distribute state film funding equally between genders (Lange 2016). In 2013, the SFI presented the action plan *Towards a Gender Equal Film Production* and launched several important initiatives to promote women in Swedish film like mentorship programmes, regional talent-development programmes with a focus on female role models and the web portal Nordic Women in Film (Kang 2016; SFI 2017b). A year later, in 2014, the SFI could present spectacular results. The share of female key staff in feature-length fiction films funded by the SFI commissioners reached 50 per cent, while the percentages for women screenwriters and women producers were even higher, 61 and 69 per cent respectively (SFI 2017a: 19). In the subsequent years, these high numbers could however not be sustained, which replicates the Norwegian experience and suggests that gender equality needs continuous effort (see Table 3 and Table 4).

Similarly, if in 2015, 57 per cent of the top five highest funded films were directed by women, in 2016, that number fell drastically to 20 per cent (SFI 2017a: 20). As the SFI

Table 3: The female shares of key staff in feature-length fiction Swedish films funded by the SFI-commissioners 2012–17.

	2012	2013	2014	2015	2016	2017
Director	32%	38%	50%	43%	65%	23%
Screenwriter	35%	46%	61%	32%	38%	22%
Producer	33%	62%	69%	44%	42%	65%

Table 4: The female shares of the top five highest funded films in Sweden 2012–16.

2012	2013	2014	2015	2016
17%	33%	40%	57%	20%

notes in their annual report from 2016, women directors make films on a lower average budget than their male counterparts and have a harder time in reaching audiences through cinema distribution, although their films receive good critical recognition (SFI 2017a: 18). In the new action plan launched in 2016, *Goal 2020: Gender Equality in Film Production*, the SFI announced several qualitative analyses and an annual film seminar focusing on gender for teachers and film educators (SFI 2017b). These initiatives promise to continue the fight to achieve lasting gender equality in Swedish film.

The gender statistics from Norway and Sweden are unmatched internationally. Although much needs to be done before achieving gender parity in Scandinavian film, the numbers of Norwegian and Swedish women behind the camera are significantly higher than what we can find elsewhere in the world. The Scandinavian films by and featuring women filmmakers discussed in this book have done their fair share in boosting those numbers. On the other hand, gender equality in film is not just about the numbers, as the CEOs of the NFI and the SFI underline (Mitchell 2015). It is above all a matter of enabling a diversity of perspectives that reflect the entire population of Norway and Sweden. Women represent half of that population and both women and men are equally savvy film audiences. Moreover, having women's perspectives represented on screen is not just a question of basic human rights. Diversity also has a positive impact on the quality of films delivered, allowing new ideas to emerge and securing the constant development of Scandinavian film sectors.

We are at a pivotal moment in history when more and more (Scandinavian) women are starting to occupy key positions behind the camera. The Scandinavian women that make films about their own vulnerabilities partake in this change and therefore deserve attention for the diversity of perspectives they bring to the fore. If gender provides an important frame for my discussion, in this book, just like in White's, gender is not a totalizing discourse. Other frameworks like race/ethnicity, nationality, mental illness, parenthood, migration, bullying and indigenousness also play an important role. In this way, I show how the female body becomes the staging ground for dilemmas that concern men and women, Scandinavians and non-Scandinavians.

Last, but not least, there is another reason to look closer at contemporary Scandinavian films by and featuring women filmmakers. In several of the film examples discussed by White, femininity is commonly coded as emblematic of the nation. This is not always the case with contemporary Scandinavian film. In my previous research, I have shown that in contemporary Norwegian cinema, it is the male body that becomes the locus for the articulation of the love of one's nation (Dancus 2013). From this perspective, analysing how Scandinavian women filmmakers stage their own vulnerabilities in front of the camera is all the more intriguing, as these films by and featuring women challenge and deterritorialize established notions of Scandinavianness and nation at the same time that they critique globalization.

Vulnerability: Filmic exposure

Vulnerability is central to the films analysed in this book. Drawing on recent scholarship in political philosophy and ethics, I understand vulnerability to be a multifaceted, shared condition, with negative and positive manifestations, closely intertwined with regimes of power, and manifested in concrete relationships and practices (Butler 2004, 2009, 2016; Butler et al. 2016; Fineman and Grear 2013; Gilson 2014; Mackenzie et al. 2014). This definition informs all my film analyses in this book. Sometimes, I explicitly reference vulnerability scholarship, like in Chapter 1, in which I analyse Solveig Melkeraaen's film through seven types of vulnerability as defined by scholars like Judith Butler and Catriona Mackenzie. Othertimes, like in Chapter 6, I implicitly draw on vulnerability theory to discuss the many nuances of vulnerability connected to migration in Ahang Bashi's film.

Staging vulnerability through a female body, as these Scandinavian women filmmakers do in a male-dominated film industry, is a risky affair. Discourses of vulnerability have been used to marginalize and control women, with women being described as frail, weak, overly emotional and therefore in need of paternalistic protection (Gilson 2014; Mackenzie et al. 2014). Moreover, because vulnerability is an inevitable part of our embodiment (all humans are born vulnerable), some worry that it dilutes political claims into ontological arguments with little political leverage (Butler 2016). Because of this, it could be argued that the Scandinavian films in which women stage their own vulnerability run the risk of reinforcing the very paternalistic, oppressive, stigmatizing, exclusionary and essentialist discourses that have kept women at the margins of society, and at the margins of film.

On the other hand, feminist scholars have demonstrated that vulnerability can be an important resource of social transformation and resistance (Butler et al. 2016; Fineman and Grear 2013; Gilson 2014; Mackenzie et al. 2014). According to American ethicist and feminist theorist Erinn Gilson, vulnerability as a framework enables us to conceive of the self as 'reciprocally constituted by others, always fundamentally interconnected and interwoven with the selves of others, permeable, and both mutable and in the process of altering' (2014: 178). This way of thinking, Gilson argues, commits us to responding not only to our own vulnerability, but also to the vulnerability of others, as well as to problematize and critically assess the social norms that attend vulnerability (2014: 171–78). Further, American philosopher and gender scholar Judith Butler is interested in how bodily vulnerability is mobilized in forms of nonviolent resistance such as street protests that claim the right to public space and equality (2016: 26). From this perspective, vulnerability is not opposed to resistance, but in Butler's words '[V]ulnerability can emerge *within* resistance and direct democracy actions precisely as a *deliberate mobilization of bodily exposure*' (2016: 26, emphasis added).

This deliberate mobilization of bodily exposure to power is particularly interesting to assess in the context of film, a medium Butler does not discuss (her focus is on street protests such as the ones at the Gezi Park in Istanbul and the Occupy Wall Street Movement). Film projects in which women directors are simultaneously behind and in front of the camera engage in multiple and complex forms of exposure. In the *Merriam-Webster Dictionary*, there are three main meanings for the transitive verb 'expose':

(1) subject/submit to a (harmful) action or influence (like in 'expose to a disease' or 'expose photographic film to light');
(2) make known/disclose (like in 'expose a murderer' or 'expose a myth');
(3) cause to be visible/exhibit for public (like in 'expose a playing card' or 'expose oneself') .

(*Merriam-Webster Online* 2017)

In the Scandinavian films by and featuring women filmmakers analysed in this book, all these meanings of 'expose' are at play. The women filmmakers subject themselves to the camera in order to make visible social taboos. As they do that, they self-expose in ways that they cannot fully anticipate and/or control. At times, the process of filming acerbates their embodied vulnerabilities. At other times, filming vulnerability becomes a mode of resistance, as Butler shows in her discussion of street protests. These tensions between various modes of exposure are at the heart of this project (hence the title of the book), and so are these Scandinavian women filmmakers' calls to be receptive and responsive to vulnerability.

While vulnerability scholars agree on the importance of receptivity and responsiveness to vulnerability, there is disagreement as to who and how to respond to vulnerability. American legal theorist and political philosopher Martha Fineman (2013) proposes the institutionalization of a state receptive to vulnerability, an idea that the editors of the volume *Vulnerability in Resistance* remain sceptical of (Butler et al. 2016: 2). According to Fineman, vulnerability is universal, constant and particular: all individuals are born vulnerable, although experiences of vulnerability may differ on an individual level (2013: 20–21). Social, political and economic resilience, on the other hand, 'is produced over time within social structures and under societal conditions over which individuals may have little control' (Fineman 2013: 24). Given the universal and particular nature of vulnerability as well as the sociopolitical and legislative mechanisms through which individuals accumulate resilience, Fineman calls for a state that takes an active role in lessening, ameliorating and compensating for individual vulnerability. Writing from an American context, Fineman has a political goal. She seeks to replace the liberal subject with the vulnerable subject, and the neo-liberal, restrained state with a responsive state in which individuals are actively involved in monitoring that 'the state is working effectively and in an egalitarian manner' (Fineman 2013: 26).

When gauged against the Scandinavian experience, Fineman's idea of the responsive state offers some intriguing observations. Beginning with the late 1970s and 1980s, the Norwegian state became responsive to the pleas coming from the women's movement and made feminism into an important tenet in shaping public policy in connection to welfare, labour and family. In 1987, in her book *Welfare State and Woman Power: Essays in State Feminism*, the Norwegian political scientist Helga Hernes coined the term 'state feminism' to capture the alliance between the Norwegian state and the Norwegian women's movement at a time when Norway was entering a new era of economic development that required the active participation of women into the labour force. In retrospect, Hernes underlines that the term 'state feminism' was meant to be descriptive and positive (2004: 288). Accordingly, it described a Nordic feminist model that coupled political mobilization from below with political intervention from above and which advocated for democratic rights for women on parity with men, and not because of women's allegedly distinctive qualities of care and altruism (2004: 291–92).

Engaging with subsequent Nordic criticism of the notion of state feminism, like the critique advanced by the Norwegian sociologist Cathrine Holst, Hernes admits a political and cultural bias that favoured social democracy as a political model and idealized Norwegian culture as the cradle for this unique 'window of opportunity', as Hernes calls it (2002: 291). If Hernes contents herself with recognizing the cultural bias, ethnic minority women and indigenous women in Norway early on argued that the normative side of state feminism failed to take ethnic and cultural diversity into account (Predelli et al. 2012). According to Norwegian sociologist Line Nyhagen Predelli and political scientist Beatrice Halsaa, these claims 'did not lead to much debate and self-examination among majority women activists' (Predelli et al. 2012: 5). On the other hand, more recent scholarship has shown that the term 'state feminism' has accumulated negative ballast in the Norwegian public discourse in the second half of the 2000s.

In an analysis of 700 Norwegian newspaper articles in the period 2007–11, the Norwegian gender scholar Siri Øyslebo Sørensen (2014) illustrates how the term 'state feminism' is commonly used to raise discontents at how the state has failed men and minority women and to criticize the political Left in Norway for institutionalizing feminism through among others the introduction of gender quotas in administrative boards. As Sørensen demonstrates, in the media discourse, state feminism is seen to privilege the elite (already powerful, ethnically Norwegian women), which in turn enables antifeminist stands and a conservative feminism that underlines the liberty of women to choose traditional gender roles. Sørensen implicitly argues that this shift in discourse is detrimental to the feminist cause of 'equality for all' because it relies on rhetorical mechanisms such as simplifications, extreme remarks, intensification, personalization and polarization (2014: 237).

If the notion of state feminism has opened for various voices to rally against feminism in the late 2000s, it is also a fact that there are many feminist projects that coexist in contemporary Scandinavia. These projects build on the feminist legacies since the 1970s and come in response to the multicultural societies that the Scandinavian countries have become. This book attends to this plurality of voices by discussing women filmmakers with a variety of sociocultural and ethnic backgrounds: ethnically Norwegian and ethnically Swedish women, women with or without a formal film education, women with indigenous and migrant backgrounds. As already mentioned, at the centre of the book are the tensions between various forms of exposure and various (positive and negative) manifestations of vulnerability. I will show that these tensions attest to how these Scandinavian women filmmakers mobilize vulnerability in an attempt to reconfigure the cinematic, the political and the ethical.

Finally, entering into dialog with vulnerability scholars from the Anglo-American world, this book examines the notion of vulnerability in the context of film and from a Scandinavian perspective. This combined focus on vulnerability, film and Scandinavia offers new, important perspectives on vulnerability. To date, there are few critical studies that have employed vulnerability as a prism to understand contemporary Scandinavia and contemporary Scandinavian films. In the edited volume *The Power of Vulnerability: Mobilising Affect in Feminist Queer and Anti-Racist Media Cultures*, several of the contributors use historical and contemporary examples from Scandinavia, first and foremost Swedish film and TV, to discuss how the language of vulnerability has been mobilized in connection to diversity policies, lesbian citizenship and AIDS-activism (Koivunen et al. 2018). The preoccupation with the politics of vulnerability in media cultures is also at the heart of this book project, though *Exposing Vulnerability* both expands the empirical focus to include Norwegian examples and concentrates on a particular type of filmmaking at a particular time in history (films by and featuring women filmmakers in the period 2009–2016). Last, but not least, *Exposing Vulnerability* also addresses the ethics of vulnerability and how the formal aspects of the films analyzed carry ethical meaning.

Another systematic study of vulnerability in Scandinavia is the book *Loneliness and Its Opposite: Sex, Disability, and the Ethics of Engagement* from 2015, in which anthropologist and queer theorist Don Kulick and gender scholar Jens Rydström discuss what opportunities adults with significant disabilities in Denmark and Sweden have to live an erotic life. Through a comparative study, Kulick and Rydström find out that Denmark and Sweden have chosen very different ways of engaging with the sexuality of people with significant disabilities: whereas in Sweden, 'the sexuality of people with disabilities is denied, repressed, and discouraged', in Denmark, 'the sexuality of people with disabilities is acknowledged, discussed, and facilitated' (2015: 4). The empirical material in Kulick and Rydström's study consists of formal interviews, archival material and ethnographic fieldwork, a methodological choice that is motivated by the desire to produce scholarship that engages with the actual lives of specific individuals rather than abstract theorizing that loses sight of the fact that some people are more vulnerable than others (2015: 272).

Exposing Vulnerability shares Kulick and Rydström's preoccupation with documenting and understanding vulnerability in its specificity by turning attention to films by and featuring Scandinavian women filmmakers. The book argues that these films are important sites for debates on Scandinavian vulnerabilities related to phenomena such as depression, bullying, racism or migration, and therefore afford important reflections about how cultural discourses of vulnerability ramify into the sociopolitical domain.

First person cinema: Gender, cultural and ethical considerations

In the films analysed in this book, women filmmakers engage in practices of self-mediation: they put themselves and their close ones in front of the camera and stage their own vulnerabilities in connection to a variety of phenomena. Today, self-mediation has become a mass phenomenon. Selfies are an inherent part of growing up in the digital age and 'the selfie generation' is an established term in public debates. Formats like blogs, vlogs, reality TV and 'brutally honest' memoirs have become very lucrative, drawing overwhelming public attention to their authors and securing financial gain. The American star Lena Dunham, best known for writing and acting in the HBO-series *Girls* (2012–17), is a good example of this. In 2014, Dunham published her memoir *Not That Kind of Girl: A Young Woman Tells You What She's 'Learned'*, a book that stirred allegations of sexual abuse and name bashing, and sold millions, reaching second place on the *New York Times* Best Seller List on 19 October 2014 (*The New York Times* 2014). Another example, this time from Norway, is the blogger Sophie Elise Isachsen aka Sophie Elise, who has won several top-rated blog awards in Norway and who, in 2016, released her autobiographical book *Forbilde* ('Role model') and topped the list of best-paid bloggers in Norway (Østbø 2016).

Despite the obvious differences in terms of nationality (Dunham is Jewish-American, Sophie Elise is northern Norwegian), socio-economic background (Dunham is the daughter of profiled artists in New York; Sophie Elise is the daughter of a middle-class family from a small town in northern Norway), occupation (one is an internationally known actress, writer, producer and director; the other is a national blog icon) and not least body image (one has been an advocate of imperfect female bodies on screen; the other has shaped her body through extensive plastic surgery), Lena Dunham (born 1986) and Sophie Elise Isachsen (born 1994) have more in common than what one may predict at a first glance. Both subscribe to the feminist truism of making the private public and both make significant financial profit as a result of selling their personal brand. In their respective books, Isachsen and Dunham stage their own vulnerabilities in connection to body image, sex, drugs and mental illness in provoking ways, but without truly managing to explore the political and ethical potential that lies in that provocation. Instead, they both fall into predictable patterns of ego-driven narratives that do little to reconfigure the aesthetical, the political and/or the ethical.

If self-mediation has become a personal brand for young women like Isachsen and Dunham, how do Scandinavian women filmmakers engage in projects of self-mediation in the 2000s? How do they inscribe themselves in the pro-filmic world and stage their own vulnerabilities?

How do these women publicly expose themselves? These questions are particularly interesting to ask in the Scandinavian context where, as we have seen, film institutions like the NFI and the SFI are actively working to enable more female perspectives on screen.

In the introductory chapter of the edited volume *The Cinema of Me: The Self and Subjectivity in First Person Documentary*, American film scholar Alisa Lebow lists a plethora of terms that film scholars have used to describe practices of filmic self-inscription: the self-portrait film, essay film, video diary, vernacular video, home movie, autobiographical documentary, subjective cinema, auto- or domestic-ethnography, self-reflexive film and finally, first person film (2012: 2–6). Of these, Lebow favours the last term, first person film, which she treats as a mode of address rather than a filmic genre. There are at least two reasons why Lebow chooses the denomination 'first person film'. On the one hand, the term encompasses both projects that are explicitly and fully autobiographical, as well as projects that are autobiographical only implicitly and/or in part (2012: 1). On the other hand, the grammatical structure of the first person manifests singular and plural formations ('I' and 'we'), which are closely intertwined (2012: 3). Thus, Lebow writes, 'the "I" is always social, always already in relation [...] always in effect, the first person plural "we"'(2012: 3). This is important to Lebow, for as she explains, first person films not only express the individuality of their filmmakers, who speak in the first person singular, but also address a 'we', 'our commonality, our plurality, our interrelatedness with a group, a mass, a sociality, if not a society' (2012: 3).

Maintaining an academic interest in filmic self-inscription since the 1980s, Michael Renov (2008) also embraced the term 'first person film' in his later research on the topic, though he interchangeably used it with filmic autobiography. Renov's research protrudes and resonates with Lebow's discussion of first person cinema, which is why I would briefly like to mention some of his main points in conversation with Lebow. According to Renov, first person films underline the partial and contingent character of self-knowledge and, in this manner, disrupt the illusion of objectivity commonly claimed by documentary filmmaking (2008: 41). Renov welcomes this disruption for theoretical and pedagogical reasons – 'can breed a kind of healthy scepticism regarding all documentary truth claims' (Renov 2008: 41), while Lebow emphasizes its ontological value – 'it actually unsettles the dualism of the objective/subjective divide, rendering it inoperative' (Lebow 2012: 5).

Another point that both Renov and Lebow make is that first person films are nothing new. Historically speaking, avant-garde filmmakers and video artists have long experimented with first person films, yet it is first in the 1990s that self-inscription also became a prominent practice in the documentary film (Renov 2008: 44). That said, new modalities and forms of first person cinema are emerging with the advent of new technologies. Renov mentions the personal website and the blog, while Lebow lists the iMovie as an example.

Last, but not least, both Renov and Lebow dismiss the common presupposition that first person films are solipsistic and self-absorbed. Renov argues that filmmakers of first person films mobilize personal, self-reflexive narratives to focalize and contextualize political aims (Renov 2008: 47–49), while Lebow discusses how culture, ethnicity and geopolitics play out in representations of the self in first person cinema (Lebow 2012: 7). To access the various cultural configurations of the self, Lebow and her colleagues discuss examples from eleven different countries and regions spread across three continents: India, Brazil, Argentina, Palestine, Israel, Lebanon, Australia, Italy, Spain, the United Kingdom and the United States.

I draw on Lebow's and Renov's scholarship and choose the term 'first person film' to refer to the Scandinavian films by and featuring women filmmakers analysed in this book. The term 'first person film' is broad enough to accommodate various degrees of self-inscription, both explicit and implicit, fully and partially autobiographical films. It encompasses the filmmaker's individuality as well as her interrelatedness with a community, both the 'I' and the 'we'. The term addresses not only the films' formal features, but also their political and ethical dimension. For these reasons, I find the first person film to be an accurate umbrella term to describe my corpus. Having said that, this book does not stop at borrowing Renov's and Lebow's definition and simply applying it to the seven films analysed. Rather, through an in-depth analysis of these films, I seek to supplement existent scholarship on the first person film through a three-fold contribution.

First, I gender the 'person' in the first person cinema by looking at first person films made by Scandinavian women. This gendering of the first person is productive not only in the context of the male-dominated film industries, where women remain a minority, but also in relation to what the American writer David Shields (2010) has called 'the reality hunger' perceptible in contemporary art. Starting with the beginning of the 2000s, Scandinavian scholarship has avidly discussed works by Scandinavian artists, filmmakers and authors who erase the border between fiction and non-fiction (Haarder 2014; Jerslev 2004; Jerslev and Gade 2005; Knudsen and Thompsen 2002). Questions of genre and performativity are central to these inquiries, and perhaps no other author has generated more public and scholarly interest in Scandinavia, as well as abroad, than the Norwegian Karl Ove Knausgård. Knausgård's six-volume novel *Min kamp* (*My Struggle*) (2009–11) is a tour-de-force into one man's trials and tribulations, desires and nightmares, dilemmas and insecurities, everyday life and intimacies. As Knausgård has himself pointed out in interviews with the press, a recurrent theme in his novels is the anxiety to be perceived as effeminate (Anthony 2015). The Norwegian-American writer Siri Hustvedt (2016) is sympathetic of Knausgård's honesty and angst about emasculation at the same time that she condemns the sexist assumptions underlining his six-volume novel.

If discourses of gender are central to novels like *My Struggle*, gender as a prism has been less present in Scandinavian scholarship on the real in the 2000s, with a few notable exceptions. The Swedish literary and gender scholar Lisbeth Larsson has done important work on how Scandinavian female authors have used their own experiences in various forms of autobiographies (Larsson 2010, 2016). In an informative article on the online database The History of Nordic Women's Literature, Larsson (2016) gives a historical perspective on women's life writing in the 2000s by going back to the 1970s, when autobiographic narratives were an integral part of the feminist struggle. The Danish media scholar Anne Jerslev (2004) makes a similar rhetorical move in her analysis of how intimacy is staged on TV and in documentary films in the 2000s. Jerslev also underlines that intimacy has been part of the public domain since the late 1960s when women's movement mobilized under the slogan 'the personal is political' (Jerslev 2004: 21). She then argues that discourses of intimacy have however changed in the 2000s: 'one speaks in public to a larger extent as an individual, private subject, and not, like in the 1970s on behalf of a group. One speaks of oneself for oneself' (Jerslev 2004: 21).

Although Jerslev uses the feminist framework to historicize intimacy in our contemporary media cultures, her analyses do not address gender as a specific dimension of intimacy in the 2000s. This book seeks to address this lack by discussing how Scandinavian women filmmakers thrust themselves and their closed ones into the public eye not only as humans and artists, but also as women. Here, it is worth recalling Patricia White's point about how the new generation of women directors do not necessarily identify themselves with feminist activism (2015: 18). That the Scandinavian women filmmakers analysed in this book do not necessarily have a feminist agenda, it does not mean that our analyses of their works should be gender-indifferent or gender-blind.

A second contribution to the academic field of the first person film is the Scandinavian perspective presented in the book. The book argues that Scandinavian films by and featuring women directors afford important reflections on how Scandinavians culturally configure the self in the 2010s. In political science, Norway and Sweden are often described as strong, interventionist welfare states, while solidarity, consensus and trust are commonly named as central Scandinavian values (Ingebritsen 2002; Tvedt 2009; Witoszek 2011). Unexpectedly perhaps, Swedish historians Henrik Berggren and Lars Trägårdh (2006) further point out that individualism is a very strong tenet in Sweden, and Scandinavia by extension. Unlike in other parts of the world, like in the United States, for example, a strong, interventionist state is seen as an asset, and not a hindrance, to individualism in Scandinavia. Berggren and Trägårdh call this ideology 'state individualism' and track its historical roots. This book affords reflections on how the notion of state individualism permeates (or not) the first person films of Scandinavian women directors from the 2000s. In this way, *Exposing Vulnerability* brings a new cultural perspective to the 'cinema of me' as discussed by Lebow and her colleagues.

Last, but not least, I specifically consider the ethical dimension of first person filmmaking. In *Film and the Ethical Imagination*, Asbjørn Grønstad (2016) argues that films provide ethical insights not primarily through narrative (ethics as a matter of content or ethics as an encounter with others), but through the cinematic form (optics as an ethics). Favouring form over content, Grønstad uses examples such as Michael Haneke's *Amour* to demonstrate how filmic figuration generates ethical knowledge. He understands ethics as a mode of interrogation, rather than a moral system (2016: 88–90), and argues that films that cultivate openness, uncertainty and opacity are generators of ethical knowledge because they show us other modes of being (2016: 91–93). In this book, I follow suit and investigate how first person filmmaking as a mode of address provides an ethical experience not only on the level of narrative, but also on the level of form. Methodologically, this involves a penchant to close reading combined with a systematic effort to flesh out what the images do and what they make us do.

Overview of the book and analytical questions

Each of the chapters in this book delivers an in-depth analysis of one Scandinavian first person film from the 2000s, with the exception of Chapter 5, in which two Scandinavian first person films are discussed comparatively. The seven examples have been selected based on the prevalence of the topics approached by the filmmaker, as well as with an eye for the potential of these films to trigger a change of attitude, if not bring along institutional changes. To give a couple of examples, in Chapter 1, I analyse Solveig Melkeraaen's film *Good Girl*, which addresses depression as a condition that continues to be associated with social stigma, although millions of people around the globe suffer from it (WHO 2017). Chapter 6 sets the limelight on Ahang Bashi's *Fragility*, a film that criticizes clinical practice and social expectations and treats panic attack disorder as something more than just an illness.

It has also been important to attend to the formal diversity of first person films, which in turn provides a variety of ethical content. In a film like *Brothers*, the director Aslaug Holm is rarely seen in front of the camera. Instead, she speaks from behind the camera and makes extensive use of voice-over to convey her experience as a mother filming her two sons in real time for almost a decade. In *The Reunion*, the director steps in front of the camera in order to stage her own experiences with bullying. Unlike in *Brothers*, where the entire cast consists of social actors, in *The Reunion*, the director is the only one to play herself. The rest of the cast in her film consists of two teams of professional actors, a formal feature that, as I will show in Chapter 3, impacts significantly the ethics embedded in the film.

In my approach, films are more than evocative case studies that do important diagnostic work. I treat them as 'theoretical objects', to reference a concept used by the Dutch cultural theorist Mieke Bal. Borrowing the term from the French art historian Hubert Damisch, Bal (2013) explains that images are not merely illustrations of what we already know; rather, they speak back, activate thought and invite viewers to theorize. Inspired by Bal, and Grønstad, I propose that the Scandinavian first person films by women filmmakers are theoretical objects that generate theoretical content of relevance to scholars of vulnerability, first person cinema, gender and ethics. This is why I afford each film extensive narrative space, so that it can speak back and make us think. The chapters can stand on their own, with my analysis emphasizing various theoretical aspects of particular relevance to the topics engaged by the films. Together, the films analysed in this book provide a complex picture of life in contemporary Scandinavia. Versions of Chapters 1 and 4 have been published earlier, the first, in *Journal of Scandinavian Cinema* (Dancus 2016), the latter in a Norwegian anthology on the aesthetics of suffering (Dancus 2017). Both these chapters have been reworked to fit in the context of this book.

In Chapter 1, I examine how the Norwegian director Solveig Melkeraaen stages her embodied experiences with severe depression and electroconvulsive therapy (ECT) in *Good Girl*. Since its introduction in the late 1930s, ECT, proverbially known as electroshock, continues to be a popular treatment for severe depression. It is also a contested treatment, not least since a disproportionate number of patients receiving electroshock are women (Hirshbein 2012). The chapter shows how Melkeraaen remains largely confined to positive and medicalized accounts of ECT. It also shows how the shooting of the film seems to have augmented Melkeraaen's suffering rather than alleviate it, which makes this film a case of what Lauren Berlant (2011) calls 'cruel optimism' and defines as an attachment to fantasies and desires that undermine the very aim that inspired them.

Chapter 2 draws attention to parents' need to document the lives of their children in a digital age. It analyses the Norwegian film *Brothers*, in which we see the director Aslaug Holm filming her two sons for almost a decade. In *Boyhood* (2014), Richard Linklater constructs a fictional framework around the growing up of his protagonist Mason (Ellar Coltrane). In *Brothers*, Holm follows no manuscript when documenting the growing up for her own children. Instead, she is completely attuned in the present, with her camera always at hand to record in real time. As small children, Holm's sons treat the camera as a substitute mother of sorts. But the older the boys get, the more reluctant they become to be part of their mother's film project. The chapter discusses how Holm goes about documenting the life of her children and whether her cinematic treatment affords viewers any ethical reflections. In addition to a discussion of *Brothers*, the chapter also presents a comparison to a similar project from the United States, Doug Block's *The Kids Grow Up* (2009), in which the director films his daughter for more than ten years.

In Chapter 3, I analyse the Swedish performance artist Anna Odell's debut film, *The Reunion*. Scandinavia is internationally known for actively addressing bullying in schools and for developing some of the most successful anti-bullying programmes in the world. In *The Reunion*, Odell describes personal experiences that do not match this reputation. In the film, Odell comes out as a victim of bullying and stages an epic backlash when she confronts her old bullies as grown-ups. This chapter discusses the innovative strategies used by the director to stage her embodied experiences with bullying. These include dramatizing a hypothetical class reunion and re-enactments of conversations Odell had with her former classmates. The chapter also shows how the film disrupts the viewer's ethical investment in a (re)constructed universe highly controlled by the director.

Chapter 4 brings attention to self-harming through a discussion of the Norwegian film *Ida's Diary*. Because self-harming is often kept hidden, it is hard to accurately assess the prevalence of this behaviour. However, Norwegian experts estimate that one in ten Norwegian youth self-harm (Helsedirektoratet 2014). They also argue that self-harming behaviour is most prevalent among teenage girls and that it is highly contagious (Helsedirektoratet 2014). In *Ida's Diary*, we get acquainted with Ida Storm, a young Norwegian woman who has filmed her own fight with mental disorders and self-harm. In 2009, Storm sent her film material to the film company Indie Film and the Norwegian director August Baugstø Hanssen was given the mandate to tell Storm's story in what five years later became *Ida's Diary*. The collaboration between Storm and Hanssen is intriguing in many respects. If Hanssen is the director of this film, Storm stands for starring and filming. On the one hand, Hanssen treats Storm's video material in ways that seek to avoid the social contagion of self-injury that experts warn about. For example, he chooses not to show the self-harming itself, only the consequences of it, and mobilizes a set of aesthetic devices that make the viewer interact with Ida's emotional pain rather than observe her scars from a distance. On the other hand, the film fails to reflect on Storm's five-year long collaboration with the film team and the camera's ambivalent role in relation to the exposure Hanssen and Storm initiate. The last point is worrisome, given the fact that the film especially targets youth.

In Chapter 5, I investigate how women directors with Sami indigenous background expose their Sami identity as they set up to shoot a family documentary. Starting with the late 2000s, several women directors have made films in which they step up in front of the camera to stage and assume their Sami identity. This is quite unique given the histories of discrimination that the indigenous Sami have suffered at the hands of the Norwegian and Swedish majorities. One of the dire consequences of this systematic discrimination has been that several generations of Sami have grown up with a ravaging sense of shame about being Sami. By making films about their own Sami identity, these women directors seek to confront and transgress that shame. This chapter takes a closer look at this group of women directors whose indigenous background makes them a minority within a minority. It analyses Ellen-Astri Lundby's *Suddenly Sami* and Yvonne Thomassen's *My Family Portrait* in which the directors assume their Sami identity in real time, so to speak. The chapter shows how biological and genetic discourses are mobilized in the process of becoming a Sami. Historically speaking, this turn to biology and genetics presents us with a cruel paradox. At the turn of the century, Nordic scientists were heavily engaged in measuring, psychologizing and racializing the Sami body (Kyllingstad 2014). This is poignantly shown in the critically acclaimed Swedish feature *Sameblod* (*Sami Blood*) (Kernell, 2016). If *Sami Blood* gives a historical perspective on racialization in a fictional format, this chapter seeks to discuss why the recent turn to biology and genetics as witnessed in the two Norwegian first person films mentioned above is problematic.

Chapter 6 takes up the subject of panic and migration through a discussion of the Swedish film *Fragility* by Ahang Bashi. For several decades now, many refugees have made Sweden their home. Bashi belongs to a generation of Iranians who fled Iran in the 1980s and grew up in Sweden. In *Fragility*, she sets out to investigate her own struggle with panic disorder and depression. In the process, she uncovers traumatic experiences of migration that her family has tried to put behind after moving to Sweden, and which Bashi cannot remember because she was too young when her family left Iran. The film affords a productive comparison to other films discussed in the book, in particular *Good Girl* analysed in Chapter 1 and *Suddenly Sami* and *My Family Portrait* analysed in Chapter 5. Both *Good Girl* and *Fragility* discuss depression, but while *Good Girl* is largely committed to medicalized accounts of ECT, *Fragility* takes up the psychosocial stress connected to the trauma of migration. Moreover, just like the Sami women directors discussed in Chapter 5, Bashi represents a minority within a minority: she is a woman with migrant background.

Finally, in the Conclusion, I return to the various types of cinematic figuration provided by my corpus and emphasize how the Scandinavian films by and featuring women filmmakers are a call to responsiveness. I highlight how these films speak of Scandinavian experiences with configuring the vulnerable self in the 2010s and also clarify how the reflections put forward in this book are relevant to a global audience.

The broad analytical questions guiding this book are the following:

- How is vulnerability imagined and staged in the chosen films?
- How do the staged vulnerabilities resonate across the public sphere and perform political work?
- How do these staged vulnerabilities operate as an ethical resource for the viewers?

Chapter 1

Good girl gets electroshock[1]

Depression is a common condition in our postmodernity, with more than 300 million people around the globe being affected by it (WHO 2017). Despite its high prevalence in all age groups and effective methods of treatment, depression continues to be a taboo in our societies, and few depressed patients dare to speak publicly about their mental struggle. In the Norwegian film *Flink pike* (*Good Girl*) (2014), the director Solveig Melkeraaen decides to confront the social stigma of being depressed by making a film about her own severe depression. *Good Girl* is an explicitly autobiographical film in which the director resorts to the first person film as a mode of address in order to investigate the causes of her mental struggle and in an attempt to interrelate with all those who are directly or indirectly affected by depression.

On the night *Good Girl* was shown for the first time at the 2014 Bergen International Film Festival, the movie theatre was packed to the brim, with expectant guests filling not just the seats, but also the two stairways on the side. After the screening, Melkeraaen was expected for a round of Q&A and I was one of the eager audience members. As *Good Girl* started to unfold, the film's tagline – 'a feel-good film about depression' – kept coming back to me. To my puzzlement, the deeper we got into the film narrative, the more improbable the promised feel-good experience seemed and I gradually became uncomfortable. When *Good Girl* reached its dramatic climax, a scene in which the director receives electroconvulsive treatment (ECT), familiarly known as electroshock, my discomfort and displeasure accelerated; I started feeling unwell and I instinctively turned my eyes away from the screen to the audience around me. Many were in tears, some in shock, yet some others looked fascinated and curious. I also noticed that the large majority of the audience were women in their twenties and thirties, most of them in the same age group as Melkeraaen and myself. Later, as I re-watched the film several times, I always came back to my visceral reaction at the film's premiere in Bergen as well as to the reactions of the audience around me. Why did this first person film engender such strong responses?

In order to answer this question, I analyse the film through the notion of vulnerability, a condition that Melkeraaen stages by sharing her own embodied experiences with depression and ECT. My analysis is threefold, with a focus on the aesthetics, politics and ethics of vulnerability. First, Melkeraaen utilizes collage as an aesthetic strategy to stage vulnerability and experiment with the first person film when she intertwines a variety of cinematic techniques spanning from highly stylized scenes of her fantasies to raw footage of her receiving ECT. Second, vulnerability opens up ways to question the celebrated image of gender egalitarianism in Scandinavia by turning the spotlight on the 'flink-pike' (good girl) debate in Norway. In the film, Melkeraaen presents herself as a good girl who wanted so much that she became severely depressed, but who finally learned to cultivate 'the art of not giving a damn' (Aasheim 2014). I argue that the cultural politics of *Good Girl* evince what American cultural theorist Lauren Berlant calls 'cruel optimism'. According to Berlant, '[a] relation of cruel optimism exists when something you desire is actually an obstacle to your flourishing' (2011: 24). *Good Girl* shows that Melkeraaen's solution, to not give a damn, is in fact cruelly optimistic, affirming and profoundly threatening at the same time. Third, a focus on vulnerability in Melkeraaen's film makes evident the ethical dilemmas engendered by first person films that take up taboo mental states like depression and contested treatment methods like ECT. I begin with a theoretical discussion of vulnerability as multifaceted, on which my reading of *Good Girl* relies.

Vulnerability: A complex and ambiguous condition

In daily discourse, vulnerability is commonly read as a weakness that opens up to potential harm, violence, stigma, pain, and patronizing social control. Neo-liberal capitalism encourages the pursuit of invulnerability as 'a desirable character trait and form of subjectivity' (Gilson 2014: 75), frames the vulnerable subject as purely a victim (Fineman 2013), and constructs vulnerability in opposition to resistance (Butler 2016). Such approaches operate with a one-dimensional understanding of vulnerability as an exclusively negative condition to be denied and disavowed. Yet, feminist thinkers remind us that vulnerability is much more complex and ambiguous, manifesting different forms.

In the introduction to *Vulnerability: New Essays in Ethics and Feminist Philosophy* (2014), Australian scholars Catriona Mackenzie, Wendy Rogers and Susan Dodds distinguish five types of vulnerability: inherent, situational, pathogenic, dispositional and occurent. While the first three refer to sources of vulnerability, the last two describe states of vulnerability. Inherent vulnerability is a basic structure of the human condition whose sources 'arise from our corporeality, our neediness, our dependence on others, and our affective and social natures'. Situational vulnerability is context sensitive and refers to experiences manifested in concrete relationships and practices. The authors further underline that inherent and situational sources of vulnerability are not categorically distinct, for 'ultimately all vulnerability is experienced in the body, whether its source is inherent or situational'. Meanwhile, pathogenic vulnerabilities are a subset of situational vulnerabilities that 'may be generated by a variety of sources, including morally dysfunctional or abusive interpersonal and social relationships and sociological oppression or injustice' (Mackenzie et al. 2014: 7–9). In a separate contribution to the volume, Mackenzie gives an example of pathogenic vulnerability: when measures intended to ameliorate inherent or situational vulnerabilities end up exacerbating the sense of powerlessness of those whom the measures target (2014: 39). Further, the introduction also differentiates between different states of vulnerability. While dispositional vulnerabilities 'are not yet or not likely to become sources of harm', occurent vulnerabilities 'require immediate action to limit harm' (Mackenzie et al. 2014: 8).

In her work on vulnerability and precariousness, Butler further implies a distinction between perceived and marked vulnerability in order to capture how structures of power deploy the vulnerability discourse to produce difference and achieve dominance (Butler 2004, 2009; Butler and Gambetti 2013). Perceived vulnerability is in fact an established concept in health care, also known as perceived susceptibility. It 'reflects an individual's belief about the likelihood of health threat's occurrence or the likelihood of developing a health problem' (Gerrard and Houlihan 2008). If in health care, perceived vulnerability is commonly used to predict health behaviours and how patients process health information, in Butler's work, it encompasses beliefs about the likelihood of threats related not only to health, but also to our social, economic and political lives. Marked vulnerability, on the other hand, refers to the unequal distribution of vulnerability whereby some populations are marked as vulnerable while others are seen as invulnerable or even negligible (Butler 2004, 2009). Keeping in mind these seven categories, let us identify the forms of vulnerability that are apparent in *Good Girl*.

Seven faces of vulnerability in *Good Girl*

Melkeraaen, born in 1978 and raised in Øksnes, a small municipality in Vesterålen, northern Norway, is a prolific filmmaker. Since graduating from the Norwegian Film School in Lillehammer in 2004, she has directed more than ten films, both shorts and features, primarily documentaries, but also short fiction. TV documentaries such as *Begavede barn* ('Talented children') (2006), *Statistikk* ('Statistics') (2008), and *Fabelaktige Fiff og Fam* ('The fabulous Fiff and Fam') (2009) have brought Melkeraaen public and critical acclaim in Norway as well as abroad. In 2014, she received the Edith Carlmar Prize, an award in memory of the first Norwegian woman director that recognizes a professional woman in the film sector who 'has shown integrity, the boldness to think innovatively and the will to break with convention' (NFI 2014). In *Good Girl*, Melkeraaen turns the camera towards herself and functions as both director and main character, Solveig. Note how I use the director's first name 'Solveig' to refer to the character in the film and her last name 'Melkeraaen' to refer to the director of *Good Girl*. This distinction between director as a character in the film and director as the artist behind the camera is not categorical, since the two roles blend into one another. On the other hand, the distinction affords analytical precision, which is why I also use this method in the other chapters of the book.

Of the Norwegian first person films analysed in this book, *Good Girl* is the most expensive production, financed by the Norwegian Film Institute (NFI). Melkeraaen and her team received a pre-grant of almost 5.1 million NOK, and the production budget was nearly 7.9 million NOK (Nermoen 2017). *Good Girl* was realized under the umbrella of the talent programme New Ways to Long Films, launched by the NFI in 2012. This financing programme targets directors with a clear artistic vision in the hope to stimulate 'more personal and original' film projects (NFI 2012). *Good Girl* was shown in Norwegian cinemas across the country, ranking sixteen out of the thirty most seen Norwegian films in Norwegian cinemas in 2014, with a box office of almost 23,000 tickets (Film & Kino 2014: 11). In addition, the film was distributed to more than a dozen film festivals and was broadcast on the Norwegian public channel NRK. *Good Girl* received the Audience Award at Bergen International Film Festival in 2014, a nomination in 2015 for the Dragon Award for Best Nordic Documentary at the Göteborg International Film Festival and the jury's special distinction in 2016 at the European Film Festival Integration You and Me.

Melkeraaen was one of the first directors to participate in the talent programme, taking the personal film narrative to new levels of exposure when she decided to make an explicitly and fully autobiographical film about her own vulnerability to depression. As early as the prologue, seven faces of vulnerability take shape, each described in more detail as the film narrative unfolds. *Good Girl* opens with a close-up of Solveig speaking straight into the camera against the soundtrack of a song from a ballerina jewellery box: 'To be good at something is not necessarily a bad thing, yet it is bad when it becomes too much in one way or another'.[2] As the mirror behind Melkeraaen makes clear, this is a home recording, filmed in soft focus and soft, frontal lighting. A black-on-white intertitle follows, revealing that this is 'a film by and with Solveig Melkeraaen', in other words a clearly autobiographical first person film. As the jewellery-box-song stops, the camera cuts first to a black screen, then to a stylized extreme long shot in which Solveig, dressed in a puffy, red knee-length dress and with her hair in a characteristic ballerina bun, spins around on a pedestal placed at the edge of an empty swimming pool coated in white tiles (Figure 1). She raises her hands as the pedestal turns against a grey, cloudy sky. In the foreground of the frame, their backs to the camera, are four skinny blonde ballerinas dressed in light pink tutus and flanking a woman wearing a black suit and a wide-brimmed black hat. As the viewer will later discover, the woman in black observing Solveig's spins is also Solveig, as a strict avatar who instructs Solveig the Ballerina.

The soundtrack is a musical theme that resembles the jewellery box song from the previous home recording, yet with more punctuated rhythm. The camera cuts to a medium shot filmed from below of Solveig the Ballerina spinning around and holding her arms raised above her head in an oval shape. A series of photographs of Solveig when she was young follows; diplomas, medals and newspaper clips that show her achievements. These items are clipped onto a clothesline and filmed in close-up in a one-take right pan. The pan fades into a white screen followed by a black screen revealing the title of the film in white capital letters: *FLINK PIKE* (*GOOD GIRL*). The following shot is also a close-up: Solveig is sitting in the same room as in the first home recording, but now wearing no make-up, placed in the right corner of the frame. There is no extradiegetic sound, only Solveig speaking directly to the camera: 'A while ago, I got seriously depressed, then I was hospitalized in an intensive care psychiatric ward, and then I received electroshock treatment and then I got healthy again'.

In the prologue, most evident perhaps are the situational vulnerabilities (context specific, manifested in concrete relationships and practices) connected to what Norwegian media and experts refer to as the 'good girl' syndrome to which women are prone to fall victim. One of the conundrums of gender equality policies in Norway is the continued high number of sick leaves among actively working women. Statistics from the past years show that Norway has successfully managed to tighten the gender gap in the work force, with women's average monthly earnings amounting to 86.7 per cent of men's in 2017 (SSB 2018). On the other hand, according to the Organization for Economic Co-operation and Development (OECD), Norway has the highest percentage of sick leaves in the world, with Norwegian women topping the sick-leave statistics, with over 70 per cent more absences certified by doctors than Norwegian men (Egedius 2014). Why are women so over-represented in sick-leave statistics when gender policies in Norway are among the most progressive in the world? Why do women continue to get sick despite generous parental leaves and flexible work schedules that help them combine work and motherhood? These questions have aroused much public debate and academic disagreement. Although experts are still looking for definitive answers, the majority of voices agree that one factor is the good girl syndrome: that women, far more than men, become overachievers at home, at school and at work, in their private and social lives, as partners, mothers, daughters, friends and professionals.

Right from the beginning of her film, the director establishes herself as a good girl for whom things have gotten out of control. The garland of medals, diplomas, prizes and laudatory newspaper clips together with the image of Solveig the Ballerina exemplify Solveig's impulse to overachieve. In the home recording, speaking to the camera, Solveig accepts that 'to be good at something is not necessarily a bad thing', yet she suggests that her inclination became so overwhelming that she developed severe depression. To use the terminology proposed by Mackenzie, Rogers and Dodds, the good girl syndrome, as a dispositional vulnerability among women, became an occurent vulnerability in Solveig's case. What was not yet or not necessarily a source of harm turned out to be destructive for Solveig. Once Melkeraaen's vulnerability became occurent, immediate intervention was required: the family gathered to support her and medical assistance was provided in the form of medication, institutionalization and ECT.

Another set of inherent (corporeal) and situational vulnerabilities established in the opening scene is in connection to ECT, a treatment method that Solveig states helped her recover from severe depression. The interviews the director later conducts on the streets of Oslo clearly show that the public knows little about ECT and regards it with suspicion and disapproval, not least given the histories of pathogenic vulnerability infamously associated with this treatment. As psychiatrist and ECT practitioner Claire Hilton shows, novels such as Ken Kesey's *One Flew over the Cuckoo's Nest* ([1962] 1973), adapted for the screen by Miloš Forman in an Academy Award–winning production from 1975, or Janet Frame's *Faces in the Water* ([1961] 1980) have helped disseminate this negative view (Hilton 2007). A more recent example that likewise propagates a negative perception and that resonates with younger audiences is Darren Aronofsky's film from 2000, *Requiem for a Dream*, an adaptation of Hubert Selby Jr's novel ([1978] 1996) of the same title.

Despite its bad reputation in the public imagination, ECT is in fact used in many psychiatric clinics in Norway, although few talk openly about it. In *Good Girl*, Melkeraaen attempts to demystify and normalize this treatment by bridging the two forms of vulnerability identified by Butler: the marked and perceived vulnerabilities of patients who have received electroshock. To do this, she records family conversations in which she confronts her parents about their fear to go public about her condition and their unwillingness to openly admit that her grandmother also received ECT as a young woman. She also includes an interview with her doctor at Lovisenberg Psychiatric Clinic in Oslo, who speaks warmly of the treatment. While working on the film, Solveig becomes seriously ill again and requires a new series of ECTs. In one of the treatment sessions, she brings in a camerawoman, who documents the entire procedure before, during and immediately after the electroshock. This scene, to which I will return, represents one of the emotional peaks of the film as well as a narrative climax that is resolved in the epilogue. Because this epilogue punctuates Melkeraaen's film project thematically as well as aesthetically, I will now use it to discuss the aesthetic strategies the director employs and which I argue are motivated by the ambiguity of vulnerability.

The aesthetics of vulnerability: A difficult balancing act

In the film's epilogue, after watching the recording of her ECT session together with her partner, Melkeraaen, in voice-over, shares what she has learned:

> Maybe it's true that your best traits can also become your worst ones. It's all right to be good, but not if it's about others' expectations. It's good to be in control, but not if it becomes a neurosis. It's good to give of yourself, but not if you lose yourself. I work at finding a balance, but have learned to live with the fact that I can lose it. I also work on saying nice things to myself. For instance, that there are many stories about who I am. This is how it is for all of us. Here, for example, I haven't mentioned that I had a goldfish that died right away. That I don't know whether I want to have children, but love being an aunt. That sometimes I don't feel like meeting people at the coffee shop. That I'm clearly a late riser. That I love talking a lot on the phone while drinking a lot of coffee and smoking a lot of cigarettes. Or that spinning around while looking down into the empty pool made me anxious. But my psychologist says that it's not perfection but imperfection that makes us love other people and other people love us.

The voice-over is heard over a montage of twelve stills, mostly of Solveig. The first four are medium close-ups of Solveig's reflection in the bathroom mirror. She wears no clothes on her upper body, her hair is down and she holds a camera in front of her face, covering her nose and left eye. In the first still, she looks down, in the second, to the right, then up and finally, straight into the mirror and through the mirror's reflection into the camera she holds in her left hand. As Solveig mentions that she practices saying nice things to herself, a fifth still pops up on the screen, a complex display of images arranged in concentric circles. They resemble patterns seen through a kaleidoscope. At a closer look, one discovers that all the images are in fact of the very camera Solveig holds in the first four stills, this time reflected in the mirrored facets of a disco ball. Seven other stills follow: one of a goldfish in a pool; three medium close-ups, one of Solveig holding a baby, the other of Solveig drinking coffee and the third of Solveig hiding under the duvet; and finally, three high-angle stills, one of Solveig sitting outside, talking on the phone next to two cups and a pack of cigarettes, and two of the film crew on the set.

In the epilogue, just as in the rest of the film, the filmmaker uses collage as an aesthetic strategy to problematize what it means to be vulnerable: not merely susceptible to potential pain, loss, social control and stigma, but also resilient, evasive, creative and even controlling. Just as the epilogue assembles a selection of images that the director comments on in voice-over, *Good Girl* as a whole is a collage of various representation forms in which the real and the fictional are woven together into a hybrid narrative that underscores the ambiguity of vulnerability. The film narrative constantly swings between control and lack of control, engagement and disengagement, distance and closeness, the biographic and the staged, always at risk of losing that balance.

This difficult balancing act is evident in other first person works that Danish literary critic Jon Helt Haarder groups under the label 'performative biographism'. Using examples from late modern Scandinavian literature, Haarder defines this term as follows: 'a broad cultural stream that consists of artists (and other producers of culture) who use themselves and others in an emphatically aesthetic interaction with the reader's and the public's reactions' (2014: 102–03).[3] Haarder further claims that performative biographism is written on paper as well as on the flesh, with real authors using themselves in ways that call for the reader's reaction outside the artistic realm. Some of the primary tools to push reception beyond aesthetic contemplation are the exercise of self-hatred and what Haarder calls the biographical abject and the terror of embarrassment: 'on the one hand, one can barely manage to read these descriptions that involve real people, and on the other hand, one experiences them precisely because they are over the top, strongly and undoubtedly authentic' (2014: 118).

The biographical abject, as Haarder defines it, is present in *Good Girl*, this time written on Melkeraaen's flesh. As already mentioned, viewers witness raw images of Solveig receiving ECT. As the medical personnel take control of Solveig's body, the camerawoman is left to record the ECT session. We see Solveig's body shaking in spasms immediately after the electrical stimulus is delivered, goose bumps on her skin, her toes shaking in reflex, saliva pouring out of her mouth as she is rolled onto her side, her confused, empty eyes as she wakes up from the anaesthetic.

Woven together with this raw footage are stylized fictional scenes in which Solveig's inner life and fantasies take a dramatic, personified form bordering on satire and the absurd. Five of these fictional scenes revolve around a swimming pool and two scenes cover Solveig's success in the media, one after winning an Oscar in Hollywood and the other as a guest in a talk show hosted by the Norwegian pop culture expert and trend commentator Per Sundnes. In the swimming pool narrative thread, as established in the prologue, there are two embodiments of Solveig: Solveig as a curvy ballerina dressed in a puffy red dress and spinning around on a pedestal at the edge of an empty swimming pool, and Solveig as a strict ballet instructor wearing a black skirted suit, a wide-brimmed black hat and red lipstick, and disciplining Solveig the Ballerina every time she fails to perform perfectly (Figure 1). In the film's epilogue, after delivering her lesson in voice-over, Solveig the Ballerina, an embodiment of Solveig the Good Girl, finally opposes Solveig the Strict Ballet Instructor and tells her to go to hell.

In between these two contrasting aesthetic approaches (raw, intimate, unpolished versus fictional, stylized, absurd, self-ironic scenes), there are a variety of other expressions: video diary of Solveig talking and crying straight into the camera, real-time recordings of Solveig and her partner (Figure 2), interviews with family members and doctors, staged dinner parties such as the New Year's Eve when Solveig's family is gathered around the table in coordinated black and red attire, toasting the improvement of Solveig's health. There are also stylized talking heads, for instance when Solveig and her partner Ravn Lanesskog lie in bed, both wearing white against white sheets, with the camera placed on a crane above them. Finally, the film also includes archival material such as pictures of Solveig and her family, voice recordings of Solveig when she was small and of Solveig in conversation with her therapist, as well as clips from Melkeraaen's earlier documentaries.

The reception of the film suggests that the stylized fictional scenes were harder to relate to, with several of the reviewers expressing uncertainty regarding the use of staged fantasies in

Figure 1: Solveig the Ballerina at the edge of the empty swimming pool. *Good Girl* (Melkeraaen, 2014). Cinematographer Øystein Mamen. 2014. Courtesy of Medieoperatørene AS and the National Library of Norway.

Figure 2: Solveig Melkeraaen and her partner Ravn Lanneskog in their apartment in Oslo. *Good Girl* (Melkeraaen, 2014). Cinematographer Marianne Bakke. 2014. Courtesy of Medieoperatørene AS and the National Library of Norway.

what was otherwise regarded as a moving film about depression (Eidsvåg 2014; Hostad 2014; Steinkjer 2014). Mode Steinkjer, film critic for *Dagsavisen*, Oslo's largest newspaper, thus writes:

> Humor, conversations, common sense and honest kicks from the closest ones ease the heavy theme, while abstract scenes of dancers in an empty pool or giant tooth brushes give visual input to the thematic content. It is unlikely the film is better because of the latter. (2014: 33)[4]

Terje Eidsvåg (2014) from *Adresseavisen*, from whom I borrow the title of this chapter, is in agreement with Steinkjer. He describes the scenes of Solveig receiving ECT as 'heavy stuff' and writes that the stylized scenes of Solveig's fantasies 'do not always work', although they 'contribute to a dynamics and a distance that the film perhaps needs' (Eidsvåg 2014).

This indicates that the more controlled and self-ironic the film narrative and aesthetics got, the less emotionally engaging it became. On the other hand, the raw footage of Solveig receiving ECT drew overwhelming public attention, with reviewers in agreement that it was a laudable example of personal courage to put ECT and serious depression on the public agenda (Bertheussen 2014; Linga 2014; B. Sørensen 2014). This type of response is not so much an indication of the director's failure to master collage in the first person film, as it suggests the viewers' difficulty to respond to the ambiguity of vulnerability, which in *Good Girl* involves both control and lack of control, engagement and disengagement, distance and closeness, fiction and documentary, art and life, the biographic and the staged.

The politics of vulnerability: The cruel optimism of not giving a damn

In the film, the good girl syndrome is presented as the cause of Solveig's depression. A young, energetic, outgoing and prolific director with a supporting family and a loving partner collapses into deep depression because she does not know how to limit her own ambition to do even better. As one of Solveig's friends points out, even in depression Solveig aimed at perfection. In the film, we see her hectically in search of a cure, embracing a variety of techniques, from mindfulness classes to reading self-help books, going on a diet, exercising, spa treatments, romantic dinners with her partner and, finally, when the depression becomes extremely serious, choosing ECT. And while ECT may have worked on the chemistry of her brain and restored balance, Solveig argues in the film's epilogue that the other important thing she had to learn was to let go and care less. The director reiterated this in a series of talks she gave during the film's release entitled 'Kunsten å gi faen' ('The art of not giving a damn') (Aasheim 2014). In addition, the logo of the film, which could be printed on T-shirts or fabric bags, was a ballerina extending her middle finger, designed by the Danish firm Larsen et Rasmussen.

This solution, to not give a damn, underlines several conflicting facts about the good girl debate to which both Melkeraaen and the critical reception of the film eagerly referred, in an attempt to make evident the film's relevance to society. First, although the director stated during the Q&A session in Bergen that the film was dedicated to 'all good girls of both sexes', the film narrative constructs the good girl syndrome as a female phenomenon. There are no references to good boys who cannot set limits and become ill, despite the fact that young men top the suicide statistics in Norway (Pedersen 2015). Rather than a universal condition intrinsic to humanity, the vulnerabilities enabled by the good girl syndrome are thus specifically tied to processes of gender formation or, to be precise, womanhood.

Second, the film reduces the over-representation of women in sick-leave statistics to an individual matter that can be best addressed through a change of attitude: i.e. of wanting too much, learning how to not give a damn. And while Melkeraaen advocates this approach, former Minister of Labour (2012–13) and current leader of the Norwegian Labour Party's Women's Network, Anniken Huitfeldt, implies that women should get better at the art of endurance. According to Huitfeldt (2012), women share a culture in which they encourage each other to take sick leaves, in contrast to male employees who have learned to clench their teeth and show up at work even on a bad day. Melkeraaen's and Huitfeldt's quite disparate solutions to the good girl syndrome show how women themselves reproduce cultural and political discourses according to which women are expected to cope and adapt by transforming themselves.

Third, the film brushes over a work culture in the film industry that in the words of Marjo Valve, Film Commissioner at the Finnish Film Foundation, 'may periodically require twelve-hour workdays and is therefore difficult to combine with normal family life' (Lundberg 2014). While affecting both men and women, this culture sustains the gender gap in the Scandinavian film sectors (see Introduction). In this context, it is particularly interesting to look at Melkeraaen's film not just as a performative biographic project and a first person film about depression, but also as a narrative by and featuring a female director in a male-dominated film industry.

Good Girl touches on this issue at several moments. While one of the fictional scenes depicts Solveig as an absurdly successful woman (an Oscar-winning director, a happy partner and a mother of several biological and adopted children), it becomes clear that Solveig has a challenging job in the scenes where she talks to her doctor at Lovinsenberg Psychiatric Clinic and her psychotherapist. Discussing the possibility of relapse and preventive measures, the doctor says: 'You have a job that is not exactly eight to four and it will most likely be difficult for you to set yourself the limits that are needed'. Likewise, the psychotherapist concludes that 'you have more to do than most people'. None of the reviewers of the film picked up on these otherwise peripheral comments, nor did the release of the film lead to a discussion of work culture and the position of women in the Norwegian film sector. Solveig's partner Ravn Lanesskog is in fact a scriptwriter himself, and *Good Girl* shows that his support is instrumental in Melkeraaen's recovery, but also of importance to her career as a filmmaker. Although the film presents Lanesskog first and foremost as Melkeraaen's partner and not in his professional role, one could claim that his presence could have facilitated a debate about how men in the film industry are not solely a problem. Men who support women directors and their perspectives can be part of the solution to gender bias just as much as women are.

Finally, Solveig's relapse, requiring a new series of ECTs, one of which is filmed, presents viewers with a discomforting paradox: what started as a project to understand severe depression and find balance leads to more depression and instability. Melkeraaen the Director loses control over Melkeraaen the Patient, who delivers a medical account of depression in which ECT is seen as the only real option to restore balance and control over her life. In the film, love, creativity, community, psychotherapy and alternative medicine fail to deliver, and ECT becomes the only feasible solution.

What do these four conflicting observations suggest about the politics of vulnerability at work in *Good Girl*? Inspired by Lauren Berlant, I contend that Melkeraaen's film demonstrates cruel optimism. In Berlant's discussion, cruel optimism is an affective attachment to unachievable fantasies of 'the good life' (e.g. upward mobility, job security, meritocracy, political and social equality and durable intimacy) that impedes the very aim that inspired them. Although these fantasies exhaust the subject, letting go of them is seen as more unbearable than clinging to them (Berlant 2011: 27). This, in turn, leads subjects to engage in practices of self-interruption, self-suspension and self-abeyance, which Berlant documents throughout her book.

The making of *Good Girl* paradoxically binds Solveig to a situation that is at once profoundly threatening and affirming. The director's relapse while working on the film puts her, and her film project, at major risk. At the same time, continuing filming, even during the ECT session, affirms that she is alive and creatively active. If Melkeraaen's goal is to come to grips with the good girl syndrome and the depression triggered by it, the film project ultimately shows that not giving a damn is overly optimistic, unachievable and cruelly impeding. Good girls remain attached to the fantasies of the good life (in *Good Girl*, successful career and durable intimacy in particular, but also motherhood). Again and again, they wear themselves out, at the same time choosing not to let go, constantly switching between numbness and panic. In this light, the staging of vulnerability in *Good Girl* is not so much an exercise of self-control and transformation as it is a practice of self-interruption, self-suspension and even self-abeyance. The fact that Melkeraaen mobilizes the first person film as a mode of address, and in a cultural sector where narratives by women remain relatively scarce, only makes the cruel optimism of not giving a damn more incoherent, even toxic. The very existence of *Good Girl* in a male-dominated sector is optimistic, at the same time that Melkeraaen stages her own implosion as she becomes increasingly depressed.

The ethics of vulnerability: An overtly positive and medicalized account of ECT

Despite good results on certain groups of patients, ECT remains a contested treatment method. Reputation is one of its problems. As Hilton shows, the collective unconscious and mythology of ECT disseminated through literature and film is predominantly negative. Although today ECT is administered by consent, under anaesthetics and with muscle relaxants, it is mainly associated with indiscriminate, punitive and coercive use, pain and fear of electricity (Hilton 2007). Furthermore, specialists disagree about risks and benefits, in particular the short- and long-term effects on cognitive performance (Hirshbein 2012; Rose et al. 2003). There is also a significant gap between the subjective accounts of former patients, who report loss of memory and a sense of self, and ECT practitioners, who by and large dismiss patient accounts as fuzzy and unscientific (van Daalen-Smith 2011; Hirshbein 2012). Finally, as Hirshbein points out in her historical overview of ECT, 'one of the most enduring aspects of ECT treatment over the years has been the greater preponderance of women among ECT patients' (2012: 162). According to Hirshbein, women's over-representation in ECT statistics is one of the reasons ECT practitioners, mostly men, have resisted patient complaints about memory (Hirshbein 2012: 162).

In an attempt to put ECT on the public agenda and remove the stigma associated with this treatment, *Good Girl* presents us with a strikingly positive view. In a discussion with Solveig, her doctor shows his strong belief in the method, a treatment he can only hope his own doctor would have prescribed, had he been in need of it. And while the film explicitly reveals the mechanics of ECT, it gives little insight into how and why Solveig has chosen this invasive treatment method, which changes the neurophysiology of the brain, but cannot address the psychosocial stress underpinning depression. It appears from the film that ECT is a highly efficient method, a quick fix with no side effects that allows Solveig to continue her life and keep on filming.

A study conducted by Vancouver researchers Alison Orr and Deborah O'Connor on older women's experiences with ECT shows that depressed patients commonly use medical discourses to account for their personal experiences with the treatment. Analysing the narratives delivered by six women who have received ECT and recognize the stigma associated with this treatment, Orr and O'Connor conclude:

> [r]elegated to the closet by all but the medical profession it appears that there is no opportunity for these women to develop the words to talk about their experiences in any other way. They cannot question the health care team for fear of alienating and being left to struggle alone with the power of the depression. They perceive themselves as having no real options.
>
> (2005: 32)

If Melkeraaen's effort to openly discuss depression and ECT is commendable, *Good Girl* remains largely committed to the medical discourse already available to depressed patients receiving ECT. The fictional scenes in which Solveig stages her fantasies and inner life are the only notable attempts to subvert that discourse, although their primary function is to underline the cruel optimism inscribed in the film by suggesting that a good girl's worst enemy is ultimately herself.

I argue that the overtly positive and largely medicalized account of ECT in *Good Girl*, coupled with the cruel optimism of not giving a damn, inhibits and even blocks, ethical response to Solveig's immediate suffering. The reception of the film shows that the large majority of reviewers applauded Solveig's courage to be open about ECT. The film did not, however, spur critical discussion about the risks and benefits of ECT and what makes patients consent to this treatment. Strikingly few reflected on how *Good Girl* generated pathogenic vulnerability, for rather than redressing Solveig's suffering, the shooting of the film augmented it and put the director at great risk.

Conclusion

Good Girl was advertised with the tagline 'a feel-good film about depression'. Giving psychiatric diagnoses a feel-good cinematic treatment is in fact a well-established trope in Norwegian cinema in the 2000s, with the character of Elling, a man in his fourties with social anxieties and strict routines, being perhaps the epitome of that otherwise unusual connection (Dancus 2013). In *Good Girl*, Solveig's struggle is serious and painful, but the film also adopts a lighter tone enabled by the northern Norwegian humour that the director and her family share as natives of Vesterålen. In the Norwegian social imaginary, northern Norwegians are commonly seen as direct, resilient, reconciled to and poking fun at the rough life in the merciless artic climate (Aas and Zapffe [1942] 1995). The film plays on these conventional representations of northern Norwegianness on several occasions. One of the most memorable examples is a scene in which Solveig's younger siblings, Magnus[5] and Sigrid, attempt to comfort their seriously depressed sister, who anxiously awaits an appointment confirmation for a new round of ECT treatment. They are all crammed onto Solveig's sofa, with Solveig sitting in the middle. The camera is handheld and cuts from a close-up of Sigrid's profile with Solveig and Magnus sitting in the background, first to a medium shot of the two women, and then to another medium shot of Magnus. Lamps on each side of the sofa cast soft light on their faces.

SIGRID: And then it's that Friday.
SOLVEIG: And then … then I should receive ECT.
SIGRID: Yes.
MAGNUS: Ok, next Friday?
SOLVEIG: Yes.
MAGNUS: Well, well, it will certainly be a kick-start for the weekend.

They all start laughing, including Solveig, who calls her younger brother a fool. The camera movement captures their laughter in a series of three quick pans, first a right pan from Magnus to Solveig and Sigrid, then a left pan back to the brother, and finally a third right pan back to the two women. This type of gallows humour, together with the narrative curve, which winds down in an optimistic ending in which Solveig the Ballerina stands up to Solveig the Ballet Instructor, could justify the choice of the film's tagline (also regularly used in the film's reception): 'a feel-good film about depression'.

Starting from the notion of vulnerability as a multifaceted condition, my analysis has painted a more complex picture of Melkeraaen's *Good Girl*. When staging her depression for a larger audience, Melkeraaen moves between aesthetic extremes, from raw, intimate and unpolished footage of herself, like for example the scene in which she receives electroshock, to stylized, self-ironic footage in which she depicts herself as an absurdly successful filmmaker or an overweight ballerina who fails to perform a perfect spin. The aesthetics of vulnerability in Melkeraaen's first person film presuppose a difficult act of balance between control and lack of control, engagement and disengagement, distance and closeness, the biographic and the staged. The more narrative space Melkeraaen the Patient gets, the more difficult it becomes for Melkeraaen the Director to master that balance. Moreover, the solution of not giving a damn that Melkeraaen advocates evinces what Berlant has called cruel optimism, with the film becoming an obstacle to the very transformation Melkeraaen hopes to undergo by embarking on this project. Finally, a focus on vulnerability enables the fleshing out of the ethical dilemma embedded in the film, namely that ECT remains a contested treatment to which Solveig resorts not only to cure her depression, but also to finish her film.

Notes

1 I borrow the title of this chapter from a film review written by Terje Eidsvåg (2014) and which is symptomatic of the Norwegian reception of Solveig Melkeraaen's film *Good Girl*.
2 This and all the following translations from the film are my own.
3 This and the following translation from Haarder are my own.
4 This and the following translations from the Norwegian media are my own.
5 Magnus Melkeraaen is not a new face on the screen. In 2014, he participated in the reality TV series *Farmen* (*The Farm*) (2001, Norway: TV2), an international TV format originally from Sweden in which twelve people live on a farm and compete for the title of 'Top Farmer'.

Chapter 2

Big parent is watching you

The children who grow up in the digital age are the most documented generation in the history of humankind. Together with documentation comes an unprecedented parental need to share photographs and videos of children, not just with immediate family, but also with extended online communities on Facebook and in the myriad of mummy and daddy blogs. While new as a broad social phenomenon, the practice of thrusting one's own children into the public eye is a recurrent theme among visual artists. Sally Mann is perhaps one of the best known and controversial maternal photographers. In her project *Immediate Family* (1992), Mann photographed her own children in ambiguous ways that called into question children's psychic and sexual innocence. Mann's provocative photography stirred a storm of reactions, from admiration and praise to contempt and disgust.

According to American art historian Anne Higonnet (1998), the controversies surrounding Mann's project are symptomatic of a shift in the visual history of childhood. Higonnet argues that Mann's project, together with the work of other controversial visual artists such as Robert Mapplethrope and Nicholas Nixon, indicates a crisis of the ideal of childhood innocence born out of the Enlightenment project and consolidated throughout eighteenth-century elite painting and nineteenth-century popular genre painting. She shows that the conditions of this crisis are inscribed in the very ideal of absolute childhood innocence, which builds on a paradoxical desirability: 'Children could only become desirable if they were genuinely believed to be innocent. Innocence itself became an object of desire' (1998: 132). By the late twentieth century, the meanings of children's bodies in photographs became vulnerable to dangerous sexualization and commercial exploitation, and the ideal of childhood innocence entered a full crisis. With the advent of social media, this vulnerability is further exacerbated when parents create a digital footprint of their children that can be easily misused in the present as well as in the future (Geddes 2014).

If Higonnet stops her visual history of childhood at the end of the twentieth century and limits her material to photographs of children, in this chapter, I am interested in investigating how the medium of film partakes in the crisis of childhood innocence. Given the purpose of this book, I propose the examination of first person films in which the directors film their own children growing up in real time. In these partly autobiographical films, the directors assume a double role: to film their children as part of an artistic project and to be a parent at the same time. The primary example I use is *Brødre* (*Brothers*), a film from 2015 by the Norwegian filmmaker Aslaug Holm. I compare Holm's *Brothers* to Doug Block's *The Kids Grow Up*, released in the United States in 2009. In my research, I have also come across a Russian film, *Anna ot 6 do 18* (*Anna: 6-18*) (Mikhalkov, 1994), in which the director asks his own daughter Anna to answer the same questions every year from 1980 to 1991. Mikhalkov edits these intimate interviews with his daughter together with newsreel footage from the same years when the questions were answered, so that Anna's growing up becomes a prism through which to reflect on the sociopolitical changes in the Soviet Union in the same decade. In *Brothers* and *The Kids Grow Up*, on the other hand, the focus remains on the director's children rather than on grand narratives of nation. This directorial decision to keep the universe of the film small and intimate makes particularly evident the ethical content generated by the cinematic exposure of real children in first person filmmaking. I therefore choose to limit my analysis in this chapter to *Brothers* and *The Kids Grow Up*. I concentrate on the Norwegian film, not least because the primary scope of this book is to discuss films by and featuring Scandinavian women filmmakers.

Compared to other first person films discussed in this book, *Brothers* and *The Kids Grow Up* distinguish themselves in several respects. First, the parent directors commonly interact with their children from behind the camera, and not in front of it. At the same time, the films make extensive use of voice-over to signal the parent director's presence. Also, the filming stretches over many years, commonly a decade or so, which makes these projects incredibly demanding for the director and their families. I analyse *Brothers* and *The Kids Grow Up* from the perspective of the many forms of vulnerabilities they entail and which concern the interactions between parent/director and children/main characters on the one hand, and film project and film viewers on the other. Before providing a close reading of the films, let me begin with some reflections on film ethics in relation to first person filmmaking.

Privacy, intimacy and vulnerability: Ethical reflections

Parenting and childhood on social media have sparked many debates. As demands from parents become increasingly higher, social media have been seen to play an important role in connecting parents who are in search of solutions and in need of a community. In this context, social media have become a second opinion not only to confirm the child's talents and achievements, but also to address parents' insecurities about a variety of topics spanning from questions of child rearing to health. At the same time, concerns have been raised in regard to the problem of consent, autonomy and child privacy. To what extent do parents have the right to thrust their children into the public eye? Can and/or should parents obtain informed consent from their own children before posting images and stories of them? How does the posting of intimate family moments affect the future of those children? These questions have become stringent and authorities across the globe, Norway and the United States included, have yet to address the privacy ethics for children online.

Meanwhile, in film, there has been an on-going discussion about the ethics of projects in which directors turn the camera towards themselves and their families. Although not specifically addressing the visual representation of real children, these debates are directly relevant to the ethics of film projects like *Brothers* and *The Kids Grow Up* and in which parent directors make films about their offspring. Unlike journalists, filmmakers do not have a written code of ethics by which they need to abide. Nevertheless, they are keenly aware of their ethical responsibility in relation to the subjects of their films as well as in relation to their audiences, sharing unarticulated general ethical principles, like 'Do no harm', 'Protect the vulnerable', 'Honour the viewers' trust' (Aufderheide et al. 2009).

American film scholars John Stuart Katz and Judith Milstein Katz (1991) note that films about oneself and one's family, and which they call 'autobiographical', represent a special case when questions of ethics are concerned. This is because the starting point of such films is 'a level of trust and intimacy never achieved or even strived for in other films' (Katz and Katz 1991: 210). Katz and Katz use four variables of film ethics to discuss autobiographical projects: consent (informed, voluntary), disclosure (appropriate, voluntary), motive ('using' people for a good cause), and construction (the use of reflexive strategies to make the viewer aware that this is a film made by a director). Starting from these four variables, Katz and Katz come to a many-fold conclusion. First, viewers put a greater responsibility on filmmakers who film their own families than on those who film strangers, because 'in our culture people are *supposed* to treat their families and friends with greater consideration than strangers' (Katz and Katz 1991: 123, original emphasis). Second, obtaining informed, voluntary consent from a family member, what Katz and Katz call 'intimate' consent, is more problematic because a family member will experience a higher pressure to cooperate with the director than a stranger (1991: 124). Third, in relation to the question of disclosure, given the intimate nature of autobiographical films, and which can make the viewer uncomfortable, there is a higher probability that viewers perceive unwillingness to disclose where none is (1991: 127). Fourth, viewers tend to be more suspicious of the underlying motives of autobiographical filmmakers, who may come across as driven by self-interest rather than by the wish to make a film larger than oneself (1991: 130). Finally, autobiographical films have a higher degree of transparency, with autobiographical filmmakers being 'more up-front than others in the recognition and presentation of their own impact on the subjects and events they film' (1991: 133). In brief terms, in Katz and Katz's discussion, intimacy 'contaminates', to use their term, our perception of the ethics of autobiographical films. This is because viewers set higher standards from the autobiographical filmmakers than from others. They also tend to project unethical behaviour on the part of the filmmaker. This, Katz and Katz argue, makes directors that film themselves and their close ones more ethically vulnerable than those who work with strangers.

Since the beginning of the 1990s, when Katz and Katz published their article, the intimate and the private have been at the forefront of our media landscapes (Jerslev 2004). Using examples from reality-TV and what she prefers to call 'intimate' (rather than autobiographical) documentaries from the late 1990s and onwards, Danish media scholar Anne Jerslev demonstrates how subjective experiences and emotions have become warrants for reality and authenticity in the media, in particular when subjectivity is tied to a traumatic event (2014: 15). The sharing of moments of intimacy with a larger public is not a new phenomenon. In fact, it dates back to the late 1960s, when women filmmakers used their life experiences as a site of self-inscription and to make calls for gender equality (Lane 2002: 9). As Jerslev shows, what is new in the media in the 2000s is the magnitude and particularization of the intimate discourse (2004: 21). In contrast to the late 1960s and 1970s, when women filmmakers used personal stories to talk on behalf of a group, today one talks about oneself for oneself, while the prominent discourse is not public and rational, but private and confessional (Jerslev 2004: 21).

Given the proliferation of spectacles of intimacy in the media, we need to ask how the ethics and the perception of ethics of what Katz and Katz call autobiographical documentaries, and what I, with Alicia Lebow (2012) and Michael Renov (2008), prefer to describe as first person films, have changed. Released in 2015 and 2009 respectively, *Brothers* and *The Kids Grow Up* afford precisely such an inquiry. Prompted by the way in which Katz and Katz couple ethics with the vulnerability of the director, I further propose to analyse these two films through the lens of the ethics of vulnerability. According to the American ethicist Erinn Gilson (2014), the ethics of vulnerability builds on two pillars: responsiveness to our vulnerability and to the vulnerability of others, and a critical disposition towards the norms that orient these responses. Starting from Gilson's definition, I ask whether the staged vulnerabilities in *Brothers* and *The Kids Grow Up* comparatively operate as an ethical resource. Do they compel ethical responses to others?

Brothers: Growing up in real time in Norway

Aslaug Holm is an experienced camerawoman and director from Norway. She has photographed more than forty films and directed ten documentaries. Among others, Holm collaborated with the Norwegian director Knut Erik Jensen for *Heftig og begeistret* (*Cool and Crazy*) (Jensen, 2001), Norway's most seen documentary to date about a male choir in the arctic community of Berlevåg. For Jensen's film, Holm conducted and filmed a series of interviews with the members of the choir in an intimate atmosphere that Jensen (2015) himself acknowledges that only Holm could have created. She also directed *Oljeberget* (*The Rich Country*) (2006), a film about the Norwegian Labour politician and current Secretary General of the North Atlantic Treaty Organization (NATO), Jens Stoltenberg. In *The Rich Country*, Holm follows Stoltenberg closely for a period of two years on his travels throughout Norway to gather votes for the Norwegian Labour Party in the 2005 parliamentary elections. In *Brothers*, Holm mobilizes her skills as an experienced documentarian with a keen eye for the intimate; this time to depict her own sons.

The Norwegian Film Institute (NFI) supported the making of *Brothers* with 2.5 million NOK (Nermoen 2017). The film was distributed through cinemas in Norway and Denmark. It is not often that a Norwegian documentary gets cinema distribution in Denmark, a Scandinavian neighbour that otherwise boasts an international film reputation yet to be matched by Norway. This speaks of the film's appeal outside Norway's national borders. In

Norway, the box office was almost 11,900 tickets, which places the film on the seventeenth place in the top thirty most seen Norwegian films in 2015 (Film & Kino 2015: 12). In addition, *Brothers* was shown at more than forty film festivals in Norway and abroad, and received several important distinctions and prizes. For example, in 2015, *Brothers* was awarded Norway's most prestigious film prize, an Amanda in the category of Best Director (the first time a documentary project has won this prize). In 2016, the film won the main prize at Taiwan International Documentary Film Festival and the top prize at the Hot Docs Canadian International Documentary Film Festival. The wide distribution and the critical recognition of Holm's film are a proof of *Brothers* 'worldliness', to reference Patricia White's discussion of women's cinema as world cinema (see Introduction). For despite the fact that the universe of *Brothers* may seem small and local, the film travelled far and wide, touching a cord in Norwegian as well as international audiences and critics.

For almost ten years, Holm took footage of her two sons, Markus and Lukas. *Brothers* is a selection made out of 450 hours of raw material in which we see Holm's sons grow up in the spotlight of their mother's camera. The film is a family drama literarily speaking. Holm functions as director, camerawoman, editor and mother. Her husband is the film's producer and also appears in the film as the boy's father, while her two sons, Markus and Lukas, are the main characters. When her youngest son Lukas turned six and Markus, nine, Holm started to film them everywhere and on most occasions: at home and at school, in the bathroom and in their bedrooms, on the football field and at the hair dresser's, during winter and summer, in Sagane, an Oslo neighbourhood where the boys grow up, and on Smøla, an island in the northern part of western Norway where Holm is originally from and where the family spent summer vacations (Figure 3). At the end of the film, which lasts for 101 minutes, Lukas is thirteen and Markus, sixteen (Figure 4).

In the American film *Boyhood* (2014), the director Richard Linklater uses a similar method to Holm's when he makes a feature film that follows the main character Mason (Ellar Coltrane) and his parents for several years. In that film too, viewers can see Mason grow up in real time, from a small boy to a college student. Played by the same actors, Mason's growing up and his parents' aging are real, which increases the authenticity and impact of Linklater's film when compared to other coming-of-age features. In contrast, Markus and Lukas in *Brothers* are real children, who live in a real world and who act themselves, and not fictional characters like *Boyhood*'s Mason. This makes Holm's film a strong, and in my opinion, even more haunting cinematic experience than *Boyhood*. When shooting, Holm follows no manuscript. Instead, she must be keenly attuned into the present with her camera at hand ready to immortalize the events that unfold in her sons' lives. Plunging into her own past, Holm on different occasions in the film, but also in interviews with the Norwegian media (Mauno 2015), mentions that she comes from a family of whalers. Just like her ancestors, Holm is patient and tenacious in her work, hunting for authenticity, which to a documentarian is as big of a catch as a whale is for a whaler.

That said, *Brothers* is much more than a proof of Holm's virtuosity as a filmmaker. In addition to being the director in charge, Holm is also the mother of the two boys she is filming,

Figure 3: Lukas (left) and Markus (right) Buvarp Holm at the family's vacation place on the island of Smøla, where their mother is originally from. *Brothers* (Holm, 2015). Cinematographer Aslaug Holm. 2015. Courtesy of Fenris Film.

Figure 4: Lukas (left) and Markus (right) Buvarp Holm eight years later on the same spot on Smøla. *Brothers* (Holm, 2015). Cinematographer Aslaug Holm. 2015. Courtesy of Fenris Film.

which increases what is at stake for her when embarking on this project. 'Though time is endless for a child, for a mother it passes far too quickly', says Holm in a voice-over.[1] While her sons are still young, Holm starts to fear the physical and psychological empty room left by her children when they move out, an apprehensive feeling that psychologists call the 'empty nest syndrome'. Through filming, she seeks to freeze her sons' childhood in real time so that she can return to these moments on later occasions, again and again. In other words, *Brothers* is born out of Holm's vulnerability as a parent: a mother who anticipates an empty nest.

The film is a meditation on the passing of time as experienced by a mother whose children grow up into young adults ready to leave the parental home. It is a melancholic project insofar Holm predicts a future loss that she tries to cope with by archiving her children's life. Visually, this melancholy is underpinned when Holm frames herself as a mother from the past, who hangs bed sheets to dry outside and wears retro summer dresses. These visual metaphors aside, Holm is no traditional mother. She is the director in charge who edits an enormous amount of raw footage down to a first person film that moves in the grey zone between life and art, documentary and fiction. Holm's vulnerability as a mother as well as the filming in real time guarantee the film's authenticity, while the narrative and stylistic devices used in the film transfigure the local and the particular into a universal story of interest to more than just Holm and her family. The film's critical recognition, as well as its reception shows precisely this. For example, the Norwegian film critic Guri Kulås describes Holm's family project as follows: 'Aslaug Holm is personal, but by being an excellent cinematographer, she captures known situations and creates suggestive images in which the viewer can put her own memories and reflections' (2015: 31).[2] This shows how Holm's vulnerability as a parent enables creativity and resilience in response to anxiety and the anticipated grief once the children move out of the parental home.

On the other hand, the film is also a testimony to the unpredictability of the process of filming and the vulnerability of the filmmaker who embarks on a first person project of *Brother*'s magnitude. Thirty-two minutes into the film, Holm follows her youngest son Lukas to school. In the nine-minute sequence that follows, the narrative, but also the cinematic techniques deployed by Holm simultaneously capture and produce vulnerability, which is why I propose we take a closer look at this sequence. Lukas and his friend Leander are second graders on their way to school, and Holm follows them at their heels with her handheld camera. The boys play on the way, and the fun continues when they get into the classroom and warm up for the day with a free drawing exercise. Then, the teacher asks the class to stop drawing, to which Lukas reacts negatively. He reluctantly puts away his drawing and ignores the teacher's instruction to sit next to Noradin, one of the other classmates. Instead, Lukas walks on top of the bench placed in front of the teacher and mumbles to himself 'That cheeky, cheeky teacher'. In a pan from right to left, we see Lukas finally sit down next to his classmates. As the camera cuts from a long shot of the class sitting in a circle around the teacher to a close shot of Lukas, we hear the other children repeating in choir after their teacher the date of the day: 14 October 2008. Lukas, on the other hand, seems uninterested and disengaged. Aware of the boy's acting out, but also of the camera, the teacher first asks Lukas and Leander to stop being 'cheeky' and then announces the first activity of the day: group work in maths.

Initially intended as a fly on the wall, the camera becomes an inconvenient presence in the classroom that both children and teacher are acutely aware of. This is particularly the case with Lukas, who, when informed of the content of the next lesson, declares his hate for school and leaves the classroom in a hurry. At this point, Holm needs to abandon the observational mode with which she started to shoot and rushes after her son. She stops focusing the camera on her son, but does not stop shooting. Unfocused, random, circular shots of the corridor walls, windows and classroom door are accompanied by diegetic sound of the conversation between mother and son. It is as if Holm cannot decide which role to prioritize, mother or director. The cinematic techniques (camera movement, types of shots, framing) intensify the viewer's experience of the son's frustration and the mother's distraction at the same time that they communicate liveness as a reality-effect. For as Holm partly loses control of the camera and her son, the film viewer stays vividly attune to the conflict emerging in real time. After an aborted attempt to chase Lukas down the school corridor, Holm pins her son down in a corner and comes closer with the camera. From behind the camera, she tries to convince Lukas to get back into the classroom first by pedagogically bringing up the value of resilience 'You can't run away every time things get difficult', and then by appealing to his affection for her 'They'll blame me for your absence. Right? That would be too bad. It's bad for me. They'll think it's because of filming. They'll be angry with me'. To the latter, the son responds with an adamant defence of the mother: 'If they chew you out, I'll kick them in the dick and say "Fuck you"'. Lukas's words punctuate the strong bond between mother and child established already in the prologue of the film, but also his childishness. In his mouth, strong derogatory words carry little meaning and no action, much like the appellative 'cheeky' turned out to be a term borrowed from the adults (the teacher calls Lukas cheeky) and projected back onto them. This time, though, Holm attempts to correct her son by whispering back to him from behind the camera: 'You can't say things like this'.

A poetic montage follows: a close-up of Lukas by the window, in profile, looking out, followed by two close-ups of dead insects, one glued to the window, the other lying in the corner of a windowpane. A blowing instrument punctuates the rhythm of editing with repetitive sounds blown at equal intervals. This intellectual montage suggests the themes of entrapment and slow death, with Lukas being a vulnerable child with no place to flee. When the camera fixes a long shot of Lukas standing by the window at the end of the corridor with his back turned towards the camera, Holm starts to reflect in voice-over on perceptions of childhood across time. Here, she builds on her personal, embodied experiences as a grandchild, daughter and mother. The camera cuts to a sequence of five black-and-white photographs from Holm's family album stretching across four generations: her grandparents, her parents, herself and her children. Unlike her grandparents and parents, who taught their children to do like the adults, Holm confesses in voice-over that she sees her task as a mother to assist her sons to find their own place in the world. This is because when she became a mother, she discovered that her sons 'were complete from the start. So strong and independent'. To use the terminology developed by American scholar Bill Nichols, the prevalent documentary mode at this point is performative: the slide of personal photographs corroborated with the voice-over underscores the subjective and affective dimension of knowledge and 'how embodied knowledge provides entry into an understanding of the more general processes at work in society' (2010: 201).

Childhood to Holm is no longer just a mimetic phase in the transition towards adulthood, like it was for her parents and grandparents. It is a quest and a fully-fledged existence that the school system fails to assist. Lukas says: 'I'm fed up. There is nothing important in there. It's just 1+1, 2+2, 3+3 and so on. I know how to do that'. In this way, Holm delivers a critique of the educational system that oversees children's strength and independence and treats them as small, well-coordinated robots activated by the teachers. The vulnerability of childhood, as Holm stages it, concerns the children's completeness, and not weakness and dependence as inscribed in the ideal childhood innocence dating back to the Enlightenment, and which Higonnet (1998) talks about in her book.

Children are vulnerable to the extent those around them treat them as *becomings* rather than *beings* (Qvortrup 2009). Holm is not one of these people. In fact, she takes her sons so seriously that she dedicates an entire film project to them. When Lukas and Markus are small, the camera functions as a surrogate mother to which the sons respond readily. But the more Holm shoots, the harder it becomes for her to work on this first person film. In the sequence just narrated, the camera becomes an instigator, for it is not unlikely that Lukas reacts in the classroom not despite the camera, but precisely because of it. That is why Holm as a maternal filmmaker comes across as naïve, at best, manipulative, at worst, when she uses the very film project to convince Lukas to get back into the classroom.

By the end of the film, both boys become directly hostile to the presence of the camera, with Markus, now sixteen, demanding the mother to put it away and end a decade of intimate filming in real time. As the camera focuses ground and aerial shots of buildings in Sagane, the Oslo neighbourhood where the Holms live, we hear Markus's voice: 'I'm sick of your filming. It's driving me crazy. You're just as neurotic. You can't finish it. I mean it's a decade since you started. This is a nuthouse'. A scene later, and in voice-over, Holm reflects on why it was so hard to find a meaningful end to her film: 'Why have I been unable to complete my project in a decade? Maybe because when the film is done, it means that an era is past. And the next stage is you moving away'. To finish the film, Holm had to be able to let go and accept that her sons had grown up into young adults ready to leave the nest and use the experiences accumulated in childhood to start new journeys. This message is punctuated by the film's prologue. First, there is a sequence of two shots of Holm flanked by her sons: a medium shot taken early on in the project and a long shot taken at the end of it. In both shots, Holm wears the same retro summer dress while her sons wear only shorts. The trio stands in front of the same house on Smøla, the island where Holm is originally from. If nothing in the surroundings seems to have changed, and Holm has maintained her body figure, hairstyle and hair colour, the two boys are visibly transformed, from little boys into young men. A scene from the football field follows: the teenage boys kick ball as the father enjoys a beer in the sun. The extradiegetic music is cheerful and the tone is optimistic. The father's efforts to install a passion for football in his sons seem to have been rewarded. The mother director has secured what to a parent is priceless material (memories of her children) and has finished her film. In interviews with the Norwegian media, Holm and her husband also mention that Markus's graduation from secondary school provided a suitable closure to the project (Smedsrud 2015). As Markus was getting ready for high school, the Holms, parents and children, were finally ready to move on.

Brothers in a comparative perspective

The Kids Grow Up (2009) by American filmmaker Doug Block is a similar project to *Brothers*, both in terms of how the filming was conducted over an extended period of time and in regard to the level of intimacy between parent and child. Before making this film, Block directed and produced several documentaries, of which *51 Birch Street* (2005) is perhaps most well-known and critically acclaimed. In *51 Birch Street*, Block takes a critical look at his parents' marriage and in particular at his troubled relationship to his own father. In *The Kids Grow Up*, he documents the growing up of his daughter Lucy. Just like *Brothers*, *The Kids Grow Up* is a selection of raw material shot over an extended period of time, more exactly from when Lucy is a small child to when Lucy turns eighteen and goes away to college. The film features Lucy and Block's wife, Marjorie, who is interviewed in the film, as well as Block's two sisters, his old father and stepmother, his stepson, Lucy's French boyfriend and other parents in Block's acquaintance circle.

Where Holm structures most of her material chronologically, Block chooses to constantly jump back and forth in time, systematically superposing scenes of Lucy as a young adult with scenes of Lucy as a child. The editing is thematically motivated, showing Lucy's character traits and development, with Block setting the child Lucy in conversation with older versions of herself. For example, when young adult Lucy takes her driver's license, Block is reminded of an earlier episode when child Lucy got her ears pierced, and this motivates the cross-editing of the two scenes. In both situations, Lucy is nervous, yet masters her nerves and accomplishes what she has set up for herself: as a child, she gets her ears pierced and as a young adult, she obtains her driving license. Unlike Holm, who saw Markus's graduation from secondary school as an auspicious moment to end a decade of filming in real time, Block frames his film narrative as a response to Lucy's graduation from high school: 'Now that Lucy is leaving so soon, the idea [to make a film] has taken on a whole new urgency', he says. As a result, Block intensifies his filming, closely following Lucy in her last year at home before going away to college in California.

If Holm's explicit focus is to encapsulate the experience of being a child, with occasional reflections on generational shifts and ideas of childhood, as could be seen in the sequence with Lukas at school, Block is particularly interested in exploring ideas of fatherhood. In voice-over commentaries and interactive talking heads with his old father, his wife Marjorie, his step-son (who has just become a father himself) and his sisters, Holm underlines that he strove to be a very different father than his own: emotionally attached and physically present rather than emotionally distant and absorbed in his own work, a buddy to Lucy rather than an all-knowing, authoritative father figure. On several occasions in the film, Block's father admits his limitations as a parent, while Block's siblings are critical of the patriarchal role their own father embraced. On the other hand, Block's wife Marjorie arrests her husband for being too attached and for having a hard time to grow up himself: 'You know I joke about your Peter Pan-complex, but I think it is true. You don't want to grow up. Yeah, in most ways, you don't want to grow up', she says when prompted by Block's encouragement to make observations about his relationship to Lucy as a father. Here, Marjorie implies that Lucy's growing up is taking a hard toll on Block not only because he is so close to his daughter, but also because he remains attached to the idea of childhood: Lucy's growing up forces Block to acknowledge that he is a grown up himself, which he won't.

In *Brothers*, Holm sees childhood as a complete and independent existence, which she wants to encapsulate by making a film about her own sons. In *The Kids Grow Up*, Block regards childhood as a transitional phase that he mourns even before it is lost. This is particularly clear when Block asks Lucy the child to recollect happy memories of her childhood. To this, child Lucy sharply replies: 'I am a child. This is my childhood'. But Block does more than mourn a future loss of childhood. He also reflects on what it means to grow up in the spotlight of the camera. He tracks back his urge to document his family to his own father, whose 8 mm family videos Block shares with the viewer. To Block, these 8 mm images of himself as a child remain 'the strongest memories I have of my early years'. Also, Holm is grateful to find a video made by a relative and which shows her grandfather catching a whale. As the small fishing vessel pulls on the pier, a 10-year-old Holm quickly passes by in front of the camera, securing the only footage Holm has of herself as a child. As she pauses the film on her image, Holm confesses in voice-over: 'Over 30 years later, I see my image, captured by him for a few seconds. A precious moment that reminds me of who I am and where I come from'.

Block's and Holm's filming of their own children marks a significant quantitative and qualitative change from back in the days when the camera recorded brief moments of special and happy occasions. Lucy, Markus and Lukas are not just in the spotlight. They are also under surveillance, constantly exposed by their parents' camera. In that regard, Block confesses in voice-over: 'One way I got to know Lucy is by documenting her life on camera. She had the great misfortune to be born at the dawn of the consumer camcorder and the double misfortune to have a documentary filmmaker as a father'. While his wife Marjorie ironically comments: 'She [Lucy]'ll get to see her childhood on camera and what it was like to grow up, what her dad was like. And just think when she works all this through in therapy, she can bring the footage with her. The therapist won't have to imagine what you were like'.

Both *Brothers* and *The Kids Grow Up* document that the urge to encapsulate the experience of childhood and parenthood eventually becomes an obsession for the parent and a problem for the child. An important theme in both films, the child's reticence to be part of the project takes many forms: acting out, like when Lukas kicks a bucket full of water on the kitchen floor;

refusing to answer the questions asked by the parent behind the camera, like Markus does when he is getting ready for his first class party and the mother is eager to get a confession from her nervous son; and asking the parent to stop shooting, like both Markus and Lucy eventually do. When Block starts filming 18-year-old Lucy during a Skype-conversation with a friend, an upset and angry daughter shuts her father off: 'It feels like you are asking too much of me and you're invading my privacy. And it's like stupid that you are making a film about me going away to college, but instead of having … experiencing me going away to college, you are just trying to film it'. As it could be seen in the scene with Lukas from school, being a parent and a director at the same time is a difficult act of balance. To Lucy, Block's presence as a director shooting in real time compromises the real-time experience of being a parent.

In addition to showing the reticence of the child to be filmed, both Block and Holm are transparent about the complicated matter of obtaining intimate consent when the child feels obligated to allow the parent to resume filming. After Lucy asks her father to live rather than film the experience of parenthood, Block announces in voice-over that he has decided to stop filming and that he considers abandoning the film project altogether. The confession is accompanied by footage of the city rather than intimate real-time filming or other archival clips. 'Then out of the blue and weeks after the fact', Blocks continues, Lucy leaves a message on her father's phone, which he then shares with the viewer in its entirety: 'Hi dad. I forgot to wish you a happy Father's Day. So Happy Father's Day! I love you. Thanks for being my father. Bye'. The next day, Block resumes shooting and secures footage of Lucy's last days at home. Although not explicit about what made Lucy change her mind, Block alludes that the strong emotional bond between him and his daughter is the main reason why the daughter once again allows him to film in real time and thus finish his project.

Holm's *Brothers* gives insight into a similar type of family negotiation, this time with the camera present to document the affective exchange between parent-director and son-documentary subject. Holm's older son Markus is getting ready for his first class party. The younger brother Lukas peeps through the keyhole, as Markus is meticulously fixing his hair. If Lukas has no access to the bathroom, Holm is in the bathroom together with her son and films him at eye-level in medium shots and medium close-ups as he stands in front of the mirror. The only sound is of Markus's hands brushing over his hair. After a long shot, which lasts for almost an entire minute, Markus gives up styling his hair in frustration and asks the mother to stop filming. In the next cut, Markus has put on a shirt and Holm prompts the son behind the camera to explain what will happen in the evening. Markus is visibly irritated and responds unwillingly to the mother's questions: 'It's a party. Our first class party. It's ... Why is it so important? You got to see me prepare. It's enough. Enough'. As Markus leaves the bathroom, Holm cuts to a reflection of her holding the camera in front of the bathroom mirror in a medium shot. Her facial expression suggests a mother's acknowledgement of a tensed situation. As her eyes turn to the left, the camera starts to pan in the same direction, and Markus comes back into the bathroom, this time more willing to collaborate. He says in a more reconciled tone of voice: 'I can repeat it. It is our first class party'. Holm continues to interrogate the son from behind the camera: 'Are you nervous? What are you most nervous about?'. Markus turns a profile to the camera as he leaves the bathroom and responds shortly and ironically to the mother: 'Whether there's food there'. Just like Lucy, in an attempt to preserve the affective bond to the parent-director, Markus comes back in front of his mother's camera. The pressure to cooperate with the director is high, for at stakes is not simply a film project, but the parent-child relationship. In this way, *Brothers* and *The Kids Grow Up* make evident the vulnerability of the child in front of his parents' camera.

Holm's reflections in voice-over, abrupt changes in the documentary mode (in the sequence with Lukas at school, from observational to participatory, then poetic and finally performative) and the very inclusion of scenes in which the sons refuse to be filmed, like the one of Markus in the bathroom, show how the camera is an intrusive surveillance mechanism operated by the mother: a Big-Parent-Is-Watching-You of sorts. The older Lukas and Markus get, the more we ask whether we have the right to watch. The boys' unwillingness to continue to be part of the project rubs on the viewer as we are made into uncomfortable, self-doubting surrogates of the filmmaker. After kicking a bucket full of water on the kitchen floor, Lukas refuses to talk to the mother from behind the camera. Here, the son's overreaction is no longer treated as a potentially valuable material for the film, as it was the case in the scene with Lukas at school. Rather, Holm turns the camera away, places it on the floor, and finally turns it off. To the uncomfortable viewer,[3] the black screen and the lack of sound are perceived as ethical spaces in which the child's integrity is given priority to the artistic project.

Equally reassuring are the brief moments in which Block gives child Lucy the camera and allows her to film him. Although Lucy is too young to be able to frame the subject of her camera according to her own will, she secures some accidental extreme close-ups of Block's crotch. This suggests how quickly the function of the camera can change, from a fun instrument to play with to an invasive intruder. In addition, *The Kids Grow Up* shows how Block attempts to negotiate an intimate, informed consent with his daughter. He uses control sentences: 'We haven't talked in a long time. You know how we periodically film each other'; 'I want your attention. I'll explain to you how to do this'; 'Do you have any questions about how it works?'. When Lucy turns seventeen and Block intensifies his filming, he also asks his daughter what he cannot film. 'I don't like you filming in public or going about any normal, day-to-day activities', she replies, to which Block rhetorically asks: 'But how do I show your life?' If Block systematically violates Lucy's terms, for example when Lucy talks on Skype with a friend, he is much more reserved when his wife Marjorie becomes clinically depressed. In Marjorie's case, he turns the camera off, giving the viewer the space to breathe out of the Blocks' spectacle of intimacy.

Conclusion

Analysing visual representations of children from the Enlightenment to the end of the twentieth century, Higonnet argues that the idea of childhood is undergoing a major shift, away from childhood innocence towards what Higonnet calls 'knowing children', that is children endowed with psychological and physical individuality, not merely innocent, but distinctively child-like and vulnerable (1998: 12). The first person films *Brothers* and *The Kids Grow Up* take knowing children to new levels of seriousness and exposure. Both Holm and Block attempt to encapsulate the children's independence, completeness, strength and vulnerability by filming their offspring for several years. Throughout the films, we get to know Markus, Lukas and Lucy, their character traits, likes and dislikes, hobbies and interests, emotional ups and downs, failures and successes. We see them give unconditioned love, but also negotiate the terms of the filming project when the camera becomes too invasive and controlling.

As viewers of Sally Mann's photographs of her own children, we have no insight into how the maternal photographer worked. Her photographs strike us as vague and mysterious. To use Higonnet's formulation, 'no matter how closely we look, the child remains in her own world. The more attentive the camera becomes, the more elusive the child' (1998: 210). Unlike a maternal photographer like Mann, who hides behind the camera, parental directors Holm and Block make the process of filming transparent to the viewers. Although Holm and Block step in front of the camera only occasionally, and sometimes indirectly like when Holm films her reflection in the bathroom mirror, both are very present on the sound track of the film. They either speak off-screen, from behind the camera, or comment in voice-over on the situations immortalized by the camera. The directors' presence in the film coupled with their vulnerability as parents, makes that *Brothers* and *The Kids Grow Up* are just as much about Holm and Block respectively as they are about their children. The more attentive the camera becomes, the more present and reluctant the children, and the more uncomfortable the viewing experience. *Brothers* and *The Kids Grow Up* make it clear to the viewers: vulnerability is inscribed in parenthood, in the cinematic text and in the flesh of real children growing up in real time. This invites to ethical reflections not only in regard to the directors' role as producers of spectacles of vulnerability. Also as viewers, we are encouraged to examine our own role as consumers of those spectacles. In this light, it is not so much that intimacy 'contaminates' our perception of the ethics of first person films, as Katz and Katz argued in the early 1990s. Rather, the excruciating intimacy in *Brothers* and *The Kids Grow Up* enables an inestimable ethical exercise in a digital age in which we oftentimes indulge in spectacles of vulnerability without truly embracing the ethics of vulnerability as defined by Gilson. For neither do we land a hand to vulnerable others as we would to our own vulnerable selves. Nor are we critical of the norms that orient our responses. It is upsetting, though, that this exercise goes at the expense of real children such as Markus, Lukas and Lucy and whose exposure will follow them long after their parents have finally released the film

Notes

1 This and all the following translations from the film are my own.
2 This is my translation.
3 Robert A. Clift uses the term 'uncomfortable viewing' to refer to the experience of taking pleasure in a film constructed on the displeasure of others (2014: 96–110).

Chapter 3

Bullying and the act of viewing

In the 2010s, several cases of bullying have shaken public opinion in Scandinavia. In 2013, two teenage girls from the Swedish city of Gothenburg were convicted after opening an anonymous account on Instagram where they had encouraged thousands of followers to 'slut-shame' other young people by posting defamatory photographs and comments (Bie 2013). In Norway, in 2014, at an age of 13, Odin Olsen Andersgård took his own life after years of being bullied by schoolmates (Mikkelsen and Åsebø 2014). When Odin's mother, Katrine Olsen Gillerdalen, went public about her son's suicide, the 14-year-old Villemo Hatland, a victim of bullying herself, and her mother Elisabeth took the initiative to organize a torchlight procession against bullying in Oslo in November 2014 (Åsebø et al. 2014). Others quickly followed suit and anti-bullying processions were organized across Norway, with thousands of people marching with torches through Norwegian cities and towns.

The slut-shaming case from Gothenburg and Odin Olsen Andersgård's suicide clearly show that Scandinavia is not 'the stable rock of peace and calm as it is often portrayed to be', to quote the Norwegian-Swedish psychologist Dan Olweus (2001). Born and educated in Sweden, and a research professor at the University of Bergen in Norway, Olweus has designed one of the most well-known anti-bullying programmes in the world, the Olweus Bullying Prevention Program, which is used extensively in Scandinavia, but also in other western European countries and in the United States. Olweus is a pioneer in doing research on bullying in schools since the 1970s, as are the Swedish and Norwegian governments for implementing anti-bullying legislation in the mid-1990s. Today, Scandinavia continues to be at the forefront of bullying research and Scandinavian countries like Sweden and Norway are known for financing comprehensive anti-bullying programmes and campaigns.

Although bullying statistics from the 2000s suggest that the rates of bullying are lower in Norway and Sweden than in other countries (OECD 2009, 2017b; Olweus 2001), bullying still affects negatively the lives of thousands of Swedish and Norwegian children and youth. In the 2017 Pupil Survey conducted by the Norwegian Directorate for Education and Training, 6.6 per cent of the Norwegian pupils in the age group ten to nineteen who have participated in the survey, answer that they are bullied two to three times a month or more (Udir 2018). Moreover, using statistics from the European project EU Kids Online, the Norwegian researcher Elisabeth Staksrud (2013) argues that cyberbullying is in fact more prevalent in Norway than in other European countries. In Sweden, the non-profit anti-bullying organization Friends collates statistics in the beginning of every school year that map out the prevalence and the forms of bullying in Swedish schools. In the 2018 Friends

Report, 25 per cent of the Swedish pupils (third to ninth grade) participating in the survey reported that they have been insulted by another pupil in a way that has made them feel sad, hurt or less worthy (Friends 2018: 20). Of these, 8.5 per cent reply that they have been exposed to bullying (repeated aggressive behaviour) (Friends 2018: 20).

In a public appeal held during the torchlight procession organized in Oslo in November 2014, Odin's mother expressed her hope for more effective anti-bullying measures in the future: 'I have a dream. I have a dream that all the children shall be seen, heard, and taken seriously. Odin said: "It doesn't help to tell others, they don't do anything anyways". I have a dream that no children will ever think these words' (Moen and Husebø-Evensen 2014).[1]

As also underlined by Odin's mother, increased awareness of bullying is key in addressing the problem. The Swedish film *Återträffen* (*The Reunion*) (2013) by Anna Odell does important work in raising awareness to the dynamics of bullying. A victim of bullying in secondary school, and now a profiled performance artist, Odell finds out that her former classmates organized a reunion party to which she had never been invited. In response, she makes *The Reunion*, a film structured in two parts. *Part One: The Speech* (hereon referred to as *Part One*) is the reunion party as Odell imagines it would have happened, had she been invited, and where she openly confronts her former bullies twenty years after graduation. In *Part Two: The Meetings* (hereon referred to as *Part Two*), we see Odell contacting some of her former classmates and inviting them to watch *Part One* in her studio. Four of her former classmates turn up to watch Odell's imaginary party and discuss the film together with her. Two refuse any form of contact, which makes Odell track them down at work and at home respectively, where she confronts them openly about their bullying behaviour in school.

What makes *The Reunion* a particularly provoking cinematic experience is its willingness to test the viewers' ethical borders. As attested by my experiences of using the film in various undergraduate and graduate classes in Norway, the film prompts the viewer not only to sympathize with the victims of bullying, as it is often the case in the media cover of bullying cases like Odin's for example. More importantly, *The Reunion* encourages viewers to reflect on their own position in past and present bullying constellations, and provokingly, to even question Odell's project. Consequently, as viewers, we are simultaneously enthralled by and alarmed at Odell's undertakings. To quote one of my students, 'at first, I was stunned by the geniality of this film, but the more I thought of it, the more I felt I was being deceived'. This chapter discusses the innovative strategies Odell uses to stage vulnerability by plugging into her own embodied experiences with bullying. As a first person film, *The Reunion* is explicitly autobiographical; however, as my discussion will show, the formal aspects of the film complicate significantly that autobiographical content. In my analysis, I will give particular attention to three scenes filmed as tracking shots. Broadly defined, in a tracking shot, the camera follows the action by moving forward, backward, left or right, a definition I will come back to later on in the chapter. Odell's tracking shots stand out both in terms of where in the narrative the director uses them and how she deploys this cinematic technique. The chapter also shows how the film disrupts the viewers' ethical investment in a (re) constructed universe highly controlled by the director.

Anna Odell's confronting first person art

The Reunion is Odell's debut film, for which she received a financial support of almost 3.5 million SEK from the Swedish Film Institute (SFI) through the consultant scheme in 2011 (Fröberg 2017). In an interview with *DOX: European Documentary Magazine*, Odell explains how the SFI first granted her a research stipend to develop what at that point was only a vague manuscript (Cohn 2014). This early bureaucratic commitment turned out to be a good investment for the SFI. Of the first person films discussed in this book, Odell's *The Reunion* has the largest box office. It had a wide national distribution through Swedish cinemas and broadcasting, with 178,648 cinema admissions and 865,000 TV-viewings after two national broadcasts, one in January 2015 and the other in May 2016 (Fröberg 2017). *The Reunion* was also shown abroad. It sold almost 58,000 tickets in cinema halls across Europe (LUMIERE Official Website 2018) and it participated in twenty international film festivals, where it collected important awards and nominations. At the Venice Film Festival in 2013, *The Reunion* was awarded the FIPRESCI prize for Best Debut Film in the Orizzonti section and the Fedeora Award in the International Film Critics' Week. In 2014, the film also won Sweden's most prestigious film award, the Guldbagge, in two categories, Best Film and Best Manuscript.

The generous financial support, the significant number of admissions and TV-viewings and the critical recognition Odell received for her film are quite remarkable for a directorial debut, yet not surprising for the Swedish art scene connoisseurs. In Sweden, Odell is a profiled artist, well known for *Ukänd, kvinna 2009-349701* (*Unknown, woman 2009-349701*), which was her examination project from the University College of Arts, Crafts and Design in Stockholm in 2009. The artwork highlights a recording of Odell enacting a psychotic episode inspired by her own suicidal attempt of jumping off a bridge in Stockholm thirteen years earlier. The re-enactment took place on the same bridge, but neither the passers-by nor the police, who were called to assist, were aware of Odell's artistic intentions. Alerted by the public, the police turned up at the place, handcuffed Odell and transported her to the psychiatric hospital, where she was put in restraints (legs, waist and wrists) and sedated (Backer 2009; Sauter 2012). Only the following day did Odell inform the medical personnel of the artwork, a delayed reveal that led to a storm of reactions in the Swedish public opinion and a court case against Odell (Backer 2009; Sauter 2012). Swedish theatre scholar William Sauter (2012) discusses how Odell's project is generically hard to define because it presupposes different phases: 'the enactment (on the bridge and in the hospital), the debate in the media, the trial and the sentence, the artwork as it was exhibited (before and after the trial)' (2012: 252). As Sauter points out, this generic complexity posed difficulties in court, where Odell was finally sentenced for fraudulent practice and violent resistance (2012: 256). In court, as well as in the media debate, Odell's lack of honesty became a primary concern, while the aesthetic qualities of the project, such as the hyperrealism of the enactment, were disregarded (Sauter 2012: 262).

In *The Reunion*, Odell once again taps into her past experiences, this time to stage an epic backlash against her bullies that thwarted her sense of self-esteem and aggravated her emotional turmoil as a teenager. In *The Reunion*, Odell's graduation project *Unknown, woman 2009-349701* is mentioned several times, hovering over the film narrative both as a token of Odell's national celebrity status, but also as a warning to her former classmates, whom we see unsure and even afraid of what to expect from the controversial artist's new film project. This is not to say that *The Reunion* is just a weak echo of *Unknown, woman*. On the contrary, the film bears witness of Odell's provoking first person art in which the artist willingly exposes her own vulnerability not as a way to gather empathy, but to confront established norms, disrupt existent power hierarchies and challenge aesthetic conventions.

The Reunion is a peculiar form of first person film. Odell plays herself, while the rest of the cast are professional actors. Hyperrealism becomes a trademark not only of Odell's own acting, but also of the acting of the rest of the cast, who were encouraged to use their own experiences from school and their own words to create the characters in the film in conversation with the director (Cohn 2014). The power hierarchies in the classroom were transferred to the film set, which was challenging at times since Odell functioned both as the bullied character and the director in charge. In the interview with *DOX*, Odell speaks of her collaboration with the rest of the cast:

> They [the other actors] needed to treat me as if I was a freak so that they felt fine bullying me. But then I'm also the director. To ease this process, we went back to school and acted together as if we were all 15 years old again. They could experience me not as someone they had to listen to, but be able to express this power they felt they had over me. Sometimes, it would be just me and one other person, or a small group of us, sometimes all of us together, so the relationships could be built.
>
> (Cohn 2014)

This quote shows how the performance artist Anna Odell was physically present for her team of actors in ways that other film directors cannot be. In her approach to directing actors, the real and the (re)enacted blur into one another, with Odell willingly loosening on the directorial grip for the sake of authenticity.

If in terms of acting, Odell is a virtuoso, it is also interesting to look at how Odell deploys cinematography in her film. The tracking shot is a prominent cinematic technique in *The Reunion*, with three scenes standing out for the way in which Odell uses this camera movement. All three are filmed on empty school corridors and are given extensive narrative space not only in terms of the duration of the shot, which is further accentuated by the slow-motion effect, but also in relation to where in the film narrative they occur. Accordingly, the opening scene of *The Reunion* is a tracking shot. The second series of three tracking shots appear as an intermezzo between *Part One* and *Part Two,* while the third tracking shot occurs right after Odell confronts one of her worse bullies and before the film's epilogue. In what follows, I want to look closer at these three tracking shots and use them as an entry point into a discussion of *The Reunion*. As mentioned in the introductory chapter of this book, my focus shifts from narrative to cinematic figuration and how the latter provides an ethical experience that encourages the types of interrogation and self-reflection that I have witnessed with my graduate and undergraduate students. I begin my close analysis with a brief discussion of the tracking shot as a cinematic technique and then move on to an analysis of Odell's tracking shots.

The tracking shots in *The Reunion*

In a tracking shot, the scene is filmed in one shot, with no cuts. This makes the tracking shot technically challenging, particularly if the filming involves a large cast and a set design of narrow and crooked spaces. When tracking, the camera is traditionally mounted on a cart that moves on rails, but one can also track from a moving vehicle or by using a hand-held camera or a Steadicam, which is a camera stabilizer system that allows the cameraman to precisely control the camera while moving. Because the tracking shot presupposes a double movement (the camera movement parallels the action in the frame), it gives quite dramatic visual effects that enhance the viewer's immersion in the scene often by creating tension and building suspense. If film history is full of examples of tracking shots, there are some memorable scenes that film buffs across the world immediately think of when speaking of this classical film device: the opening of *Touch of Evil* (Welles, 1958) or the scene in *Goodfellas* (Scorsese, 1990) in which the mobster Henry Hill leads his date into a nightclub through the back door. In contemporary American cinema, as film critic Jonathan Romney (2014) points out, the tracking shot has become 'a gladiatorial sport over the years, with directors trying to outdo each other and their precursors'. This can be seen among others in Alejandro González Iñárritu's *Birdman or (The Unexpected Virtue of Ignorance)* (2014), a film packed with extremely complicated tracking shots that have brought the craft of the tracking shot to new technical levels.

In a European, art cinema context, the tracking shot is not only the sign of a skilful cameraman, but also a disputed cinematic choice with a dubious ethical reputation. In 1959, in a public discussion about Alain Renais's *Hiroshima, Mon Amour* (1959), the French director Jean-Luc Godard famously exclaimed: 'Tracking shots are a matter of morality'. To him, like to other French new wavers such as Jacques Rivette and Serge Daney, the tracking shot was an intrusive and controlling cinematic technique that failed to adequately reproduce political events. The infamous example these critics used to illustrate the corruptive nature of the tracking shot was a scene from the Italian film *Kapò* directed by Gillo Pontecorvo in 1960. In *Kapò*, one of the characters in a Nazi concentration camp commits suicide by throwing herself on a barbwire fence. Pontecorvo films the death with a forward tracking shot ending in a close-up of the hand of the dead body. This cinematic choice was according to Rivette despicable, blocking intellectual distance from the great tragedy of the Holocaust. To quote the French film critic Serge Daney, the tracking shot puts the viewer '[…] in a place where we did not belong, where I […] could not and did not want to be' ([1992] 2004). If the tracking shot connotes ethical meaning, let us take a closer look at how and why Odell use this captivating, yet morally charged cinematic technique.

The Reunion opens with a tracking shot of an empty school corridor that lasts for a little more than thirty seconds. The camera tracks forward, through a glass door and straight down the corridor in slow motion at eye level. The sound is barely perceptible, undefined and strikingly void, as if heard from inside a cage: the echo of sluggish footsteps on an empty concrete floor, remote voices of children playing, an intermittent sound of what seems to be a chainsaw. The steady forward track directs attention to the green-and-white walls of the corridor, the grey floors, the white lamps, the posters and the clock on the wall. The light is natural. There are no people in the frame, and the camera tracks forward in a straight line, with no turns. The atmosphere is institutional, sterile and claustrophobic. Just as the eye becomes more observant of the *mise en scène* and the ear gets used to the strangely void soundtrack, the camera cuts to a black screen. The chainsaw sound accelerates and suddenly stops as the camera cuts again to a close-up of two arms arranging a festive table and a male diegetic voice expressing his satisfaction about how everything looks. A party is about to start. Why does Odell choose to open her film with an empty, yet claustrophobic tracking shot that places us in a close-up of a fictional class reunion that is deeply written on Odell's flesh?

The fictional reunion turns out to be the perfect arena for Odell to come out as a real victim of bullying and openly confront her bullies from secondary school. The settlement is disturbing not only because Anna is so upfront and even aggressive in tone, but also because the former classmates, now grown-ups, brush off her coming out by ignoring her charges, placing responsibility on others or counteracting her sombre stories with warm memories of solidarity, community and innocence. When Anna becomes 'too much', she is asked to leave the party, the conflict becomes physical and Anna ends up being borne out of the venue and sent home in a taxi. The atmosphere is tense. 'What a damn fool' concludes one of the classmates, 'Obviously we should have not invited everyone at this party', says one of the organizers, 'It is art', a male voice from the crowd irritably exclaims, alluding to Odell's controversial graduation project from 2009.[2] As the classmates are finally rid of Anna, the viewers can breathe somehow relieved. This is after all only fiction, a staged hypothesis: what would have happened, had Odell as a victim of bullying given a talk one would normally not give at a reunion party.

In fiction, Odell's vulnerability is re-inscribed as harmful and risky, but also therapeutic and creative. Here, vulnerability has negative as well as positive outcomes. On the one hand, this creative project gave Odell the opportunity to confront the pain she accumulated throughout secondary school and which arrested her sense of self-esteem into adulthood. As a cinematic experience, the fictional party is indeed a carefully crafted piece of fiction, filmed in close-ups, shallow depth of field, shifting focus, soft light, with an Aristotelian curve with a clear beginning, middle and end, elliptic dialog, and convincing acting and choreography. On the other hand, viewers cannot help but remark that Anna's boldness once again led to her being frozen out by her old bullies. Although she succeeds with temporarily disturbing the party, she fails to bring the bullies into self-awareness and ends up being thrown out from the party.

As Anna is put into a taxi, all the diegetic sounds are significantly toned down and replaced by a high-pitched continuous hissing similar to tonal tinnitus. This sound effect creates a sense of out-of-space-ness reminiscent of the voidness in the opening tracking shot and it allows us to dwell on Anna's emotionally charged exit. Through cinematic figuration, sound, in particular, Odell thus ties the film's prologue with the end of *Part One*. It becomes clear that the opening tracking shot transported us into a world of fiction in which Odell's vulnerability as a victim of bullying is, perhaps unexpectedly, reinforced rather than suspended. The void and institutional feel of the tracking shot stand in stark contrast to the lively conversations and the emotional temperature animating the party, yet both leave the viewers with a feeling of unpleasantness and uncertainty. Why did fiction fail to secure Odell a victory on her old bullies? What else, if not a reunion party, could have been a more effective arena for Odell to stage her backlash on her bullies?

As *Part One* ends, a series of three tracking shots transports the viewers into *Part Two*. For more than three minutes, the camera tracks on the corridors of the same school as in the film's prologue: first, a tracking shot passing lockers lined up on both sides of the wall and which have been tagged with various messages, including derogatory words such as *kuk* (cock) and *fitte* (cunt); second, a tracking shot of the same green-and-white corridor as in the prologue; and, third, another tracking from the corridor with lockers. As the camera tracks forward in a linear trajectory, we can hear Odell calling three of her former classmates (Louise, Henrik and Christopher) and inviting them to watch her new film project, a feature about a class reunion, she explains. As the last conversation with Christopher reveals, it turns out that Odell had never been invited to the real class reunion that had already taken place. That is why it is so important to her that she shows her film, i.e. *Part One*, to those classmates who were present at the real reunion. Fiction and by extension art become an instrument to the real and the ethical. As the former classmates watch the fictional party, would they recognize themselves and come to question the hierarchies that put classmates such as Odell at the bottom of the class pyramid? Would the fictional reunion prompt the real classmates to think about their own role in the actual bullying that occurred during school?

In *Part Two*, of the four that show up to watch the movie together with Anna, only Andreas seems to question his self-image and allegedly accept his role as a bully. He wants to know who he is in the film and is also interested whether what Anna says in her fictional speech is true. 'So, has this really happened? That someone fooled you that they were in love with you?', 'Did I also do it?'. When Anna replies positively to both questions, Andreas concludes: 'Yes, this is tragic'. The other three classmates fumble and avoid, deny and put blame on others as we see them uncomfortably watching Odell's fictional film in her studio and as Anna is watching them. The real creeps onto the fictional, the camera becomes more invasive and the director more confrontational. Odell's vulnerability here enables not just creativity, but also punitive action. Finally, Anna chases down two of the classmates whom she and others saw at the top of the class hierarchy: Louise at her workplace and Henrik in front of his apartment building. While the first manages to postpone a face-to-face talk to the following day, Henrik gets to hear how Anna experienced him in school: 'I remember you as one of the hardest, worst and hellish throughout the whole [school time]'. The camera is handheld, random people walk in and out of the frame. Rikard, one of the actors from the fictional party, joins Anna in the middle of her conversation and stands a meter or so behind her as she continues the conversation with Henrik. The shooting style is documentary. Henrik does not seem to be affected by Anna's accusations. Nor is he interested in having any contact with her. The conversation comes to a halt when Anna tells him that several of her classmates have noticed that he has not changed much since secondary school, a final personal attack that Henrik verbally brushes off, although his facial expression shows he is now disturbed. But before they split, Anna introduces Rikard to Henrik: 'He plays Nicke', she says. Then Henrik turns his back to the camera and goes inside his apartment building. A medium shot of Anna and Rikard standing next to each other follows. We see Anna and Rikard turning their backs to the camera and walking away. They both cast a brief glance back as if to acknowledge the presence of the camera left behind.

At this moment, a new series of tracking shots transports us back to the school. First, the camera tracks briefly on the green-and-white corridor from the film's prologue, then, it tracks on Anna and Rikard who wear the same clothes as in the scene with Henrik and who now walk down the school corridor looking at each other and inspecting the walls (Figure 5). First, they are filmed from the front, then from behind. The forward track is steady and

Figure 5: Anna and Rikard walking down the empty school corridor. *The Reunion* (Odell, 2013). Cinematographer Ragna Jorming. 2013. Copyright French Quarter Film.

in slow motion, the light, natural, the sound, just like in the prologue of *The Reunion*. As Anna and Rikard reach the stairs, they continue to walk up, with Odell leading the way. The tracking shot is discontinued and the void sound is replaced by the tunes of the avant-garde artist Laurie Anderson, more exactly 'Let X=X/It Tango' from her debut album *Big Science* (1982). The melodic line is monochrome, minimalistic and electronic. Where does this third and final series of tracking shots place us now?

First, we see a long shot of one of the actors in *Part One*, Niklas, who is sitting at a table outside a bar. He is alone, reading, with a pint of beer in front of him. The camera then cuts to a medium shot of the person observing Niklas. It is Andreas from *Part Two*, the only classmate who accepted playing a role in the bullying after watching Odell's reunion film. Andreas is in the company of three friends, but once he notices Niklas, he joins the latter at his table. It turns out Niklas played Andreas in the fictional reunion and Andreas is curious to find out more about how the actor worked with the interpretation of his character. Niklas seems quite hesitant and unwilling to talk about his acting, but mentions among others that he used Andreas's Facebook profile to gather a sense of his character.

ANDREAS: So you've been on my Facebook? So you've gone there and tried to steal my identity, haven't you? Or copy it, sort of? Like in a documentary, you try to envision me as real as possible? This is how you have worked?
NIKLAS: It makes sense that you ask about this, but at the same time I mean it is entirely my own picture of what it was that … [*Andreas interrupts him*]
ANDREAS: So you don't think it's special?
NIKLAS: No, not in this case.
ANDREAS: No, no. But it's not that you play someone that doesn't exist, like for example Darth Vader in *Star Wars* or Aragorn in *The Lord of the Rings*. You play a real person. That is special.
NIKLAS: Okay, but it is my own picture. I have my own interpretation of the person.
ANDREAS: Yes, but it is … Now the real person is here. It is as if Aragorn came here.
NIKLAS: Or not, it is …
ANDREAS: Or yes.
NIKLAS: But …
ANDREAS: I am involved in this, whether you want or not, whether I want or not.
NIKLAS: Yes, that's true.
ANDREAS: And it was exciting to meet you. It's not so often one gets to meet the actor who plays one.
NIKLAS: It's not so often that one meets a character either.

In this bar scene, the real and the fictional meet face-to-face when Andreas confronts his impersonator. Niklas is taken off-guard, struggling to finish his sentences, while Andreas seems to have the upper hand. He first alludes to a misuse of his Facebook profile: 'So you've gone there and tried to steal my identity, haven't you? Or copy it, sort of?' Then, Andreas tries to hold the actor responsible for his performance by underlying that his character is not stripped from a fantasy or science fiction film like *The Lord of the Rings* (Jackson 2001, 2002, 2003) or *Star Wars* (Lucas, 1977). Instead, the character Niklas plays is anchored in a real person, who involuntarily became part of Odell's cinematic experiment. At this point in the narrative, fiction is no longer seen just as an instrument to prompt ethical responses from the real bullies, but also as a source of ethical dilemmas for the actor who has no other choice but to deal with the real person at his table. That it is precisely Andreas who gets to meet his impersonator and question the authenticity of this performance is not accidental. After all, Andreas is the only one of the classmates to ethically respond to Odell's call in the fictional party. In the film's epilogue Andreas gets his reward: his vulnerability becomes a strength that enables him not only to respond to Odell's vulnerability as staged through fiction, but also to question the actor's performance in *Part One*.

Towards the end of their conversation, the extradiegetic tunes from 'Let X=X/It Tango' start to pick up again, making a sound bridge to the film's epilogue. The camera is now up in the sky, giving a bird's-eye perspective of the schoolyard, then, of the roof of the school, where we briefly see Anna and Rikard sitting next to each other, and finally, of houses and roads in the neighbourhood. Compared to the controlled forward tracks filmed on the school corridors, the camera movement up in the sky is more random and dynamic. As the camera gradually gains elevation, it roams around the neighbourhood for three minutes along Laurie Anderson's electronic tunes in which the synthetized voice recites verses devoid of any rational narrative. When the credits start rolling down the screen, the observant audiences who take their time to carefully read through the cast may realize that the real in *Part Two* is in fact a re-enactment, and not a documentary of the encounters Odell had with her classmates. Andreas, just like Niklas, is an actor playing a role in Anna Odell's film. As layers of fiction, reality and re-enactment start piling up on each other, it becomes evident that Odell's tracking shots place the viewers in a position to contemplate not only the vulnerability of bullying, but also the vulnerability of the act of viewing.

Odell's tracking shots are a matter of morality, yet not fully manipulative as the French wavers claimed. The tracking shots in *The Reunion* place us into the director's embodied experience with bullying, at the same time that they distance us from it. Odell is not simply a victim of bullying, she is also the creative director in charge who chases down her former bullies and asks for retribution. We support her project, but also grow increasingly uncomfortable as she becomes more confrontational and controlling, in particular at the end of *Part Two*. We believe her, but we also get confused about why and how various parties failed to perceive themselves as bullies. For in this payback project, it is no longer the bullies, but Odell the director who has the power to decide and label, which brings us to my next point.

Odell's tracking shots both open up and block formal and moral reflexivity in relation to the act of viewing. Encoded as fiction, *Part One* immerses the viewers into a brutal settlement between Odell and her former bullies, without bringing awareness to the relationship between film and viewer. Throughout *Part Two* and in particular in the film's epilogue, when Andreas reaches out to Niklas, the viewers are encouraged to cultivate awareness of the complex interactions between art and life, fiction and reality. At the same time, the delayed disclosure that *Part Two* is a re-enactment played by actors, casts doubt on the claim to authenticity in Odell's project. What is authentic and real in this first person film and who is looking at whom and how in *The Reunion*? With the understanding that *Part Two* is a re-enactment, we can conclude that Odell is looking not only at herself and her former bullies as they watch or refuse to watch her film. Odell is also looking at us, the film viewers, as we are watching her performance. With the help of the forward tracks, the director transports us from a close-up of the fictional class reunion to medium and long shots of re-enacted meetings in her studio, and finally up in the sky. Although the final bird-eye view of the school may feel liberating, in reality, it is yet another invasive shot taken from a surveillance camera controlled by the director, this time placed on a drone. As long as questions of aerial surveillance and privacy remain a hot legal potato, Odell's drone playfully sways along Laurie Anderson's electronic, senseless tunes. The drone sway is both literal, a slow movement and figurative, a controlling force.

Conclusion

In this chapter, I have discussed how *The Reunion* is a first person film in which the speaking 'I' confronts and challenges established aesthetic and social norms by mobilizing vulnerability in at least two senses: the vulnerability connected to bullying and the vulnerability of viewing.

In international scholarship, bullying is defined as 'repeated aggressive behavior in which there is an imbalance of power or strength between the two parties' (Jimerson et al. 2010: 1). The three criteria that distinguish bullying from other forms of peer aggression are thus intention, repetitiveness and imbalance of power (Olweus 2010: 11). In empirical analyses, it is common to distinguish between bullies (those who bully without being bullied) and a victim group that is divided into two categories: submissive/passive victims or victims only; and provocative/aggressive victims or bully-victims, who are both bullied and bully others (Olweus 2010:13). The majority of traditional anti-bullying programmes target the parties directly involved in bullying either as bullies, victims or bully-victims. Bullying statistics suggest that these parties are not negligible numbers, not even in Sweden and Norway, two countries that have pioneered anti-bullying measures and legislation. What has been less targeted is the majorities in the dynamics of bullying, namely those who watch others being bullied or hear about it. On anti-bullying websites, these majorities are interchangeably referred to as 'passive witnesses' or 'bystanders', despite the fact that some bullying researchers have advocated for a redefinition of the bystander as an unavoidably active and involved participant in bullying (Twemlow et al. 2004).

The 2014 torchlight processions in response to Odin's tragic death were commendable for the way in which they activated the Norwegian communities beyond the traditional dyad bully-victim. Hundreds of children and parents marched on the streets of Norwegian cities and towns in solidarity with victims of bullying and in support for increased measures to fight this destructive behaviour. With *The Reunion*, Odell pushes viewers even further. Through an innovative mix of reality and fiction, Odell couples her vulnerability as a victim of bullying with our vulnerability as viewers, and this shakes us into self-awareness. As the film credits start to roll down on the screen, we cannot but contemplate our own position as viewers in relation to the backlash staged by Odell. In the undergraduate and graduate classes I have taught, the emotional responses triggered by the cinematic figuration chosen by Odell varied from deceit to redemption, confusion, doubt or frustration. Almost immediately, students started to reflect on the complexities of power relations in a classroom and the numerous ways in which action is blocked or thwarted in bullying. It was Odell's optics that generated these types of discussions, an optics that this chapter has flashed out through close readings of Odell's tracking shots. On the empty school corridors in *The Reunion*, we meet ourselves not as passive witnesses of Odell's vulnerability, but as inevitably active bystanders in a cinematic experiment carefully controlled by the director.

Notes

1 This is my translation.
2 This and all the following translations from the film are mine.

Chapter 4

(Self)mediating self-harm

An increasing number of teenagers and young adults in the western world recur to non-suicidal self-injury, also known as self-harm, in an attempt to release psychosocial pressure and deal with stress and difficult, unresolved emotions. According to the National Health Service in the United Kingdom, the number of poisonings among girls was 42 per cent higher in 2014–15 than ten years previously, while the number of cuttings among girls almost quadrupled in the same period (Campbell 2016). A report released in 2014 by the Norwegian Directorate of Health explains that it is hard to collate precise statistics on self-harm because self-harmers often keep this behaviour hidden (Helsedirektoratet 2014). The same report writes that one in ten Norwegian teenagers of age fifteen to sixteen have self-harmed, yet the extent of self-harm may in fact be much higher than suggested by these numbers (Helsediketoratet 2014). This is because self-harmers often become part of the statistics only once their health situation has seriously deteriorated and medical intervention is required in the form of hospitalization. Also, while teenage girls and young women are over-represented in the self-harm statistics worldwide, this self-destructive behaviour is not only confined to the female gender. A survey by YouGov suggests that a quarter of young British men self-harm because of depression, anxiety and stress (Marsh 2017).

Social contagion in schools, colleges and treatment programmes is a recurrent risk factor when it comes to self-harm among teenagers and young adults (Jarvi et al. 2013). Psychologists have also expressed concern about how self-harm is depicted on the Internet, like for example in popular YouTube videos that glamorize or normalize self-harm and that give detailed descriptions of self-injuring methods without sending a clear message against self-harm (Lewis et al. 2011). Social media has further acerbated the risks associated with this self-destructive behaviour, causing alarm and despair among parents, educators and medical personnel (Borland 2016). If the latter agree that (popular) mediation of self-harm is very hard to do in an ethically sound way, they also realize that youth are active users of social media and avid consumers of YouTube and other popular culture. So how can mediation be used to engage youth without triggering, romanticizing or defusing self-harm? The Norwegian film *Idas dagbok* (*Ida's Diary*) (Hanssen 2014) offers a fascinating example to critically discuss precisely this question.

In *Ida's Diary*, we get acquainted with Ida Storm, a young Norwegian woman who has filmed her own fight against mental disorders and self-harm (Figure 6). In 2009, Ida sent her film material to the film company Indie Film and the Norwegian director August Baugstø Hanssen was given the mandate to tell Ida's story. *Ida's Diary* received pre-production grants of almost 2.1 million NOK from the Norwegian Film Institute (NFI) (Nermoen 2017) and

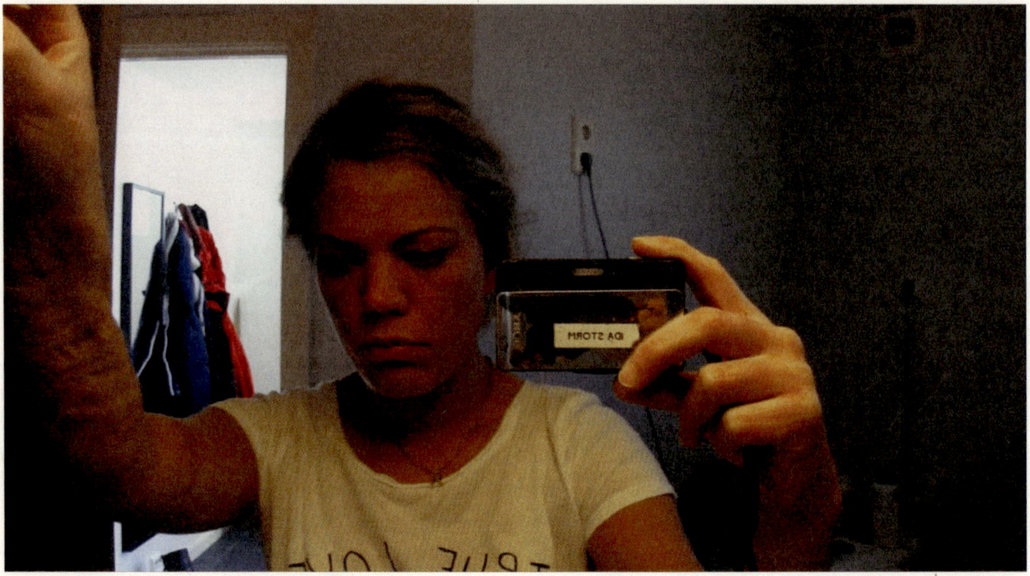

Figure 6: Ida Storm in front of the mirror with a camera in her hand. *Ida's Diary* (Hanssen, 2014). Cinematographers Ida Storm and Lars Erlend Tubaas Øymo. 2014. Courtesy of Indie Film.

it is Hanssen's debut as a solo director. If the first recordings in the film are from 2006 and 2008, most of the footage used in the film is home videos made after Ida contacted Indie Film. This means that *Ida's Diary* is a result of a five-year collaboration between Ida Storm and the director August B. Hanssen and his team.

Hanssen could take artistic control of Storm's story only because Storm pledged to film herself at her most vulnerable and was willing to entrust her video material to film professionals. Although Storm is not credited as a co-director of *Ida's Diary*, her presence in front and behind the camera is so vital to the project that I place this film under the umbrella of first person filmmaking. The mode of address in *Ida's Diary* is undoubtedly first person, while the film is a result of a partnership between an amateur filmmaker and a professional film team. In this chapter, I further investigate the nature of this intriguing collaboration by asking the following questions: How do the director Hanssen and his team artistically treat and manage Storm's raw material about her difficult mental life, and, what are the ethical challenges embedded in this process? I begin this chapter with a discussion of what type of first person film *Ida's Diary* is. I then move to a close analysis of a sequence in the film in which we see Ida self-harming for the first time. My focus in the second part of the chapter is on the filmic figuration and the ethics produced through it. In the third part of the chapter, I scrutinize the film in relation to the target audience of *Ida's Diary*, who are first and foremost teenagers and young adults. On the one hand, I show how Hanssen treats Storm's video material in ways that seeks to avoid the risks of representing self-injury that experts warn about. On the other hand, I criticize the film's failure to reflect on Storm's five-year long collaboration with the film team and the camera's ambivalent role in relation to the cinematic exposure Hanssen and Storm initiate. I find this lack of reflection disconcerting, given the fact that the film addresses youth for whom exposure in the social media is daily business.

First person filmmaking as (self)mediation

Alicia Lebow discusses how first person filmmaking is not a solipsistic endeavour; on the contrary, the 'I' also speaks in the plural by underlining its interconnectedness to others (2012: 3). A way to test whether *Ida's Diary* does indeed manage to address a 'we' in addition to expressing Storm's individuality is to look closer at the film's distribution and critical recognition. *Ida's Diary* did not have an ordinary cinema distribution in Norway, being shown at only a few places across the country and gathering a modest box office of 434 tickets sold in Norwegian cinemas (Film & Kino 2015: 36). Instead the producers at Indie Film and the distributors Tour de Force opted for an alternative distribution model for Hanssen's film. The film premiered at the International Documentary Film Festival Amsterdam (IDFA) in 2014. From there, it circulated to other international film festivals across the globe like ZagrebDox International Documentary Film Festival in Croatia, EDOC (Encounters with Other Cinemas) in Ecuador, and Helsinki International Film Festival – Love & Anarchy in Finland. In addition, the film was shown at various psychology conferences, where Storm was occasionally invited as a special guest. In 2015, Norway's largest film festival for children and youth, Kristiansand International Children's Film Festival, included *Ida's Diary* on its youth programme. The same year, the Norwegian public television NRK broadcast and streamed the film as part of a theme series about the mental health of youth, together with other critically acclaimed features and documentaries like, for example, the BBC documentary *Don't Call Me Crazy* (2013). Finally, a shorter version of the film, entitled *Being Ida*, was made available on vice.com and on YouTube, where it was seen more than 800,000 times (Urdahl 2015). Although *Ida's Diary* did not have an ordinary cinema distribution, the film's participation in the festival circuit and its distribution through broadcasting and streaming clearly indicate that Ida's story is much larger than herself. It appeals to national and international audiences, youth and adults, psychologists and lay viewers. In terms of critical acclaim, the Scottish Mental Health Arts and Film Festival awarded *Ida's Diary* the honour Highly Commended in the Feature Documentary category in 2016, while the following year, the film won the Norwegian professional award Gullroten for Best Music and Best Film Editing (Aalen 2016). These important distinctions acknowledge the interconnectedness and plurality embedded in *Ida's Diary* by affirming the artistic quality of the film and its emotional and aesthetic appeal to the public at large.

Lebow also writes that first person films are autobiographical to different degrees: while some are explicitly and fully autobiographical, others are autobiographical only implicitly and/or in part (2012: 1). *Ida's Diary* presents us with a blurry case that cuts across the pairs of distinctions instituted by Lebow. The film is at once explicitly autobiographical and autobiographical in part. Through Ida's home video footage, we get to know her diagnosis (emotional unstable personality disorder), her ups and downs, her hopes and disillusions, her small everyday victories and her destructive urge to self-harm. Ida Storm is the main character of the film as well as the provider of footage, with the camera always at hand to document her life. On the other hand, it is Hanssen, and not Storm, who has the directorial control over the narrative and filmic figuration.

It is interesting to note that the Norwegian reception of the film neglects Hanssen's artistic vision, and therefore power to form the narrative, with *Ida's Diary* being commonly referred to as a self-portrait. An illustrative example of this is when one of the Norwegian film reviewers describes *Ida's Diary* as a 'long video-selfie' in which Ida gives 'a brutally honest and revealing insight into how difficult it is to live with mental illness' (Tjellaug 2015).[1] If the term 'video-selfie' does indeed capture the intimacy factor in this film project, the word 'selfie' is highly misleading because it takes the director out of the equation. Like many of the reviews show, the film is raw and truthful, but as I will demonstrate, it is not an accidental mixture of amateur footage. Carefully chosen cinematic effects are utilized to convey an immediate intimacy that not only enthrals, but also shakes and terrifies.

The film's prologue is illustrative of the format that intimate takes in *Ida's Diary*. In the digital version streamed on the website of the NRK, the film starts with the logo of Indie Film on black screen: a cat face with long whiskers and the name of the film production house written in capital letters on two rows underneath it. The logo flashes in different yellow tones in the centre of the screen, an effect that creates a feeling of agitation and transience. We can hear that someone is walking on gravel. The logo disappears and is replaced by three intertitles with text in capital letters and using the same flashing effect like for the logo. First, 'IDA SELF-HARMED FOR THE FIRST TIME WHEN SHE WAS 10 YEARS OLD'.[2] Then, 'AS A TEENAGER, IDA STARTED TO KEEP A VIDEO DIARY IN AN ATTEMPT TO UNDERSTAND'. Finally, 'THE FILM IS BASED ON IDA'S DIARY'. On the soundtrack, we hear dangling keys, steps walking on gravel, a car door being opened. Then the steps disappear into the car and the motor starts.

A new scene is established: from behind the car wheel, a driver lifts, adjusts and places a small camera on the board in front of the windscreen. As the camera movement comes to a halt, the camera fixes a medium close-up on the driver, a young, blonde woman. It is Ida Storm, the main character in *Ida's Diary*. It is dark outside and Ida's face is illuminated in a chiaroscuro-effect familiar from the art of painting and which underlines the contrast between light and darkness. This chiaroscuro is temporarily flattened out when Ida drives by other sources of light, such as streetlights along the road or other cars in the traffic. As Ida is driving, she is speaking out loud while looking in the direction of the camera, but not directly into it:

> Ida's contact ad: Hi, my name is Ida. I am 24 years old and I miss having a boyfriend, sometimes [jump cut].[3] I have heard that I am a bit different, and, according to specialists, I am a hopeless, insane, brain-damaged former addict [jump cut]. I have emotionally

> unstable personality disorder [jump cut]. Either I love you or I hate you [jump cut]. I think Hannibal also had borderline [jump cut]. Sometimes I can be really high [*she smiles and waves one of her hands*]. Yahoo! Oh yes! That is life! Hello! Now I can live a very long time in this world! Oh, I wish it could always be like this [*she raises her voice in enthusiasm*]. Oh, yeah! Yes! And then it could go straight down [*she pushes the air hard through her lips so that they vibrate*]. Completely empty [jump cut]. To hell with the whole world! Fucking hell! [*she raises her voice in frustration*]. Erh [jump cut]. Nice if you are also like this. Or I hope you are not like me. Actually, the most important thing is that you are who you are. Yes! Sign with [*she takes a moment to think*]. Sweetie pie [*she raises her voice in expectation*]. Looking forward to an answer! Yes! Bye, bye!

When Ida says goodbye, two new intertitles are displayed in capital letters spread across the entire screen surface: first, the film's title in white-on-black text, then a transparent 2006-number on black screen through which we can see a bird's-eye view of a car parked along the road. The next scene is the first video diary entry of Ida from 2006. She sits in her car by the road and lights a joint.

There is something immediately intimate and strong, but also constructed and public about the way in which Ida presents herself in the film's prologue. Her monologue of one minute and forty seconds is an unconventional self-introduction framed as a funny contact ad. It appears to be staged for an imaginary other and not necessarily an ad meant for publication. Already from the beginning, Ida allows the viewers to come very close to her, less than an arm's length away (with the exception of the bird's-eye view seen through the 2006-number, the rest of the prologue is filmed in medium close-ups). After expressing her wish to get a boyfriend, she introduces us to her diagnoses, first in derogatory, rude appellatives ('a hopeless, insane, brain-damaged former addict'), then in the official medical jargon ('emotionally unstable personality disorder', 'borderline'). This shows that Ida can shift codes when she talks about her own vulnerability, but it also alludes ironical distance in relation to her own mental state. This irony is further built through intertextuality and a reference to one of Hollywood's most feared borderline patients, Dr Hannibal Lector known from *The Silence of the Lambs* (Demme, 1991) and *Hannibal* (Ridley, 2001) in the legendary interpretation by Anthony Hopkins. Immediately after, Ida performs her strongly labile emotional life by impersonating lines expressed by the jovial, satisfied and enthusiastic Ida followed by statements by the destructive, angry version of herself. This performance is authentic and confident, inviting and intimidating at the same time.

Stylistically, the chiaroscuro-effect underlines Ida's emotional instability by making evident her split nature: the contrast between light and darkness, black-and-white mentality, emotional extremes. The repeated jump cuts emphasize Ida's division and inner agitation. In addition, the constant shake of the camera, caused by the car's movement, interferes with the focus, making the images temporarily unclear. This underscores the imbalance and lack of foothold. But the shots are not only brutal. They are elegantly edited together with the help of the car trip as a leitmotif, which appears in the soundtrack of the opening intertitles, in Ida's self-presentation (she is driving in her car), in the intertitle displaying a bird's-eye view of a car pulled by the road through the 2006-number and finally in the first recordings from 2006 when Ida sits in her car and smokes a joint. This type of editing creates continuity in the narrative. Together with the extensive use of jump cuts, it also makes visible how Ida's strongly intimate staging is shaped by a narrative voice that controls editing, sound and cinematography. This means that the intimate in *Ida's Diary* is not raw and unfiltered, but rather mediated with artistic precision. It is at once Ida's self-mediation and a mediation under Hanssen's directorial grip, a '(self)mediation' as I choose to call it.

Ida's double confidence, first in the camera, in front of which she speaks openly and honestly, and then in Hanssen, who gets the mandate to bring her story to a wide audience, captivates us in a completely different way when compared to the intimate in reality TV shows like *Big Brother* (2001–03, 2005–06, Norway: TVNorge; 2011, Norway: TV2 Bliss; 2014, Norway: FEM). In *Ida's Diary*, it doesn't look like the main character is pushed to produce affect, as commonly seen in *Big Brother* (Jerslev 2004). On the contrary, affect oozes out of Ida. For her, being able to put words on feelings in front of the camera seems liberating and healing. Filming becomes a necessity, a support in her fight against mental illness, and not a way to fame. When she takes control of the camera, she also manages to control the difficult emotions that overwhelm her and that she otherwise releases through self-harm. Her vulnerability guarantees the authenticity of her footage, because Ida does not pretend to be sick. She does have serious problems. At the same time, she is tough, funny and ironic. When Hanssen first received footage from Ida's video diary, he was mesmerized by the potency and intimacy in Ida's vlog:

> There was something about Ida and her material that I couldn't let go. I continued to watch it. Ida is very good at translating her feelings into words. It is also something about her material that is especially captivating, I think: it is not meant for publication. In contrast to a blogger, these are films in which Ida talks to herself – it gives the material a special strength and an immediate intimacy that I noticed early on.
>
> (Stene 2015)

But how does Hanssen convert this immediate and raw intimacy present in Ida's own video recordings? To answer this question, we need to zoom into the cinematic text to a sequence where Ida self-harms for the first time.

Ida's pain and the viewer's body

Four minutes into the film, we see Ida self-harming for the first time. It is an intense cinematic experience conveyed in four minutes or so, with each minute corresponding to a new scene and a new emotional extreme. The first minute is a scene of an intoxicated Ida. In an extreme close-up, we see Ida taking a deep breath out of her joint. The floating, atmospheric mood is suggestively underlined through cinematography, music and editing. The colour tones are warm. Smoke comes out of Ida's mouth in slow motion. The focus of the camera is soft. Close-ups and extreme close-ups of Ida as a teenager and as a child are crosscut with shots taken in nature: trees in full bloom, blue-violet flowers of liverleaf, tall grass winding against a blue sky and a group of small islands. The extradiegetic electronic music reminds of ambient music with echo-filtered sound effects that are mixed together with other atmospheric chords, some percussion beats, the sound of birds chirping and/or crickets. The camera is handheld and the camera movements are so sudden that the eye can barely rest on anything. An entire repertoire of optical devices is being utilized to express the feeling of intoxication and floating subjectivity: the alternation of deep and shallow focus in the same shot, the use of blue, yellow and mauve colour filters and filters that distort the image geometrically, shots that have been exposed to the sun. Like in an echo, we hear Ida whispering, first 'This is insane', then 'Sick, sick, sick'. As she says that, she pushes the handheld camera away from her face and quickly brings it close to her face again to secure extreme close-ups of her nose and eyes. She repeats this camera movement several times.

Then, the synthesizer chords get a more metallic and darker tone. The camera cuts to a medium close-up of Ida's bare feet walking through shallow water along a beach at night. There is only one source of light in the image, most likely from a headlamp, a cold light pointing sharply on Ida's feet. The mood is disturbing. This transportation scene establishes the second scene in the sequence: a sick and debilitated Ida lying in bed. The camera cuts to two extreme close-ups, the first of a clock that ticks fast, the other of two pills dissolving in a glass of water in slow motion. The focus is on the particles that are melting into the water, while the musical chords are in a lower register and underscore the dissolving process with the help of an electronically manipulated drum loop. When Ida takes up the camera and lifts it above herself in an extreme close-up that shows half of her face from the nose up, the extradiegetic music is interrupted. Ida lies in bed and talks to the camera about being in pain, about disappointments and downfalls in school, about the numerous feelings that overwhelm her. Pop songs from a radio can be heard in the background. The camera is still handheld and the image is out of focus every time Ida adjusts her body slightly. With the help of a sound bridge that suggests that the radio connection is lost, the camera crosscuts repeated times to shots taken from a car racing at night. The footage of Ida lying in bed is filmed in soft focus and graded in soft colour tones (yellow and sepia), while the shots from the car are filmed in sharp focus and cold colour filters (blue and grey).

Two extreme close-ups, one of a foot accelerating, and the other of a hand gearing up, establish a third scene in the sequence: a literally boundless Ida that drives her car at 150 km per hour. The rhythm of the beats and the drum effects in the extradiegetic music contribute to the exhilarating atmosphere. Like from a cave, we can hear Ida commenting on the increasing speed. Extreme close-ups of the speedometer are intertwined with long and medium long shots of the road that lies ahead.

In the next scene, Ida arrives at her destination, possibly the same beach as in the transport scene that established the scene with Ida in bed. In a long shot, we can see her walking in the dark along the beach. She wears a headlamp, which makes her body throw a dark shadow on the ground. The atmosphere is dark and distorted. This establishes the last scene in the sequence, namely a desperate and confused Ida. First, we see an extreme close-up of a showerhead from which two drops of water are dripping in slow motion, then a medium close-up of a washing machine centrifuging at high speed. The contrast between the slow dripping and the fast centrifuging creates a feeling of agitation. The soundtrack is full of dissonance: the height of the tone is constantly adjusted up and down, various synthesizer effects are briefly used only to disappear again, short and sporadic chords are suddenly discontinued. Ida films herself in a medium close-up and she seems confused and frightened. 'I have no idea what to do', she says. The colour tones are yellow and sepia. The camera moves unfocused catching random shots of various furniture and objects in the bathroom and on the corridor. Glimpses of Ida's distorted face are superimposed on the shots from the bathroom and the corridor. It is as if a ghost or an evil spirit tries to break through the footage. Then the extradiegetic music stops abruptly. In slow motion, we see a strip of blood falling and dissolving into water, then an extreme close-up of a bandage that is carefully wrapped around the skin as it rustles gently in contact with it. The rustle of the bandage is the only sound in the image. Ida wakes up at the psychiatric ward at the hospital.

In this four-minute sequence Hanssen uses a cinematic language that forces us to 'watch film with the body' to cite the Norwegian gender scholar Sara Orning (2015). Orning is inspired by phenomenological film theory whereas the spectator's physical body is central to the film experience and its interpretation. Using examples from the Austrian filmmaker Michael Haneke, she shows how filmmakers like Haneke 'use the body on the screen to affect the body in the cinema hall' (Orning 2015). From this perspective, how does Hanssen use Ida's body, her old and fresh deep scars, to affect the viewer?

There is a striking tactile quality in Hanssen's images that underlines the limitations of sight and hearing. In the book *The Skin of the Film: Intercultural Cinema, Embodiment and the Senses*, the Canadian culture and film scholar Laura Marks (2000) introduces the concept 'haptic visuality'. She starts from the distinction between optical and haptic images introduced by the art historian Aloïs Riegl and builds on Riegl's terminology to distinguish between optical and haptic visuality. Whereas the first invites the viewer to scrutinize things in depth, the latter forces the viewer to use her eyes as an organ of touch that moves on the surface of the image and treats it as a type of skin (Marks 2000: 162). Optical visuality encourages the viewer to focus, investigate and contemplate forms, while the haptic visuality lets the viewer only glimpse and sense between different types of textures. Marks further underlines that the two forms of visuality are not mutually exclusive; on the contrary, we need and use both to different degrees according to the situation in which we find ourselves (Marks 2000: 163). In the sequence from *Ida's Diary* discussed above, but also otherwise in the film, the haptic visuality is prevalent. Rather than being pulled inside the cinematic illusion with the help of optical visuality, Hanssen chooses close and extreme close-ups, distorted, grainy, unfocused and overexposed images that do not allow the eye to dwell on and penetrate through the image.

It is not only the images that have a haptic quality. The same holds true of the sound and the editing. In her book, Marks is primarily interested in images, but she mentions briefly that also 'sound operates along a dialectic similar to that of haptic and optical visuality' (2000: 182–83). The sound design in *Ida's Diary* underscores the intimate, but also the painful cinematic experience. Ida's lines are unclear. She whispers and mumbles. The microphone from the camera rustles against her clothes and her body. When Ida races her car along the road, there is an echo in her voice, as if she speaks from another world or the other side of a long tunnel. Diegetic and extradiegetic sounds glide into one another to emphasize Ida's intoxication, pain, discomfort and confusion. Sound effects like bird chirps, percussion beats, steps and fast clock-ticking are mixed together with diegetic sounds like Ida's lines, radio music, noise from the traffic, the sound of the accelerating motor, the centrifuging washing machine and further with the electronic chords especially composed by Stein-Johan Grieg Halvorsen and Eyvind Andreas Skeie at Topscore. In this mixed sound environment, the ear is not allowed to listen to specific sounds, only move on the surface and gather sound impressions.

The editing complements the accelerating rhythm in the music and the multisensory cinematic experience. The camera crosscuts back and forth between Ida's amateur footage, in which she speaks straight into the camera, and stylized images of nature and blue and grey filtered images of the road. In addition, in the last scene in the bathroom, we grasp superimposed glances of Ida's distorted face. These stay on the screen only briefly so that the eye can notice them, but quickly disappear and come back intermittently.

The haptic quality of cinematography, sound design and editing puts the viewers in the position to *interact* with Ida rather than observing her from a distance. As viewers, we feel Ida's pain and scars on our own bodies. We become vulnerable to the film. Hanssen never shows us how Ida self-harms. Instead, he creates a cinematic room that resembles Ida's body, soul and heart. This is a painful room to inhabit, both for Ida, and for the viewers. The latter feel urged to give Ida a hug and tell her that everything will be all right, but they are also terrified by the self-destructive force that takes over Ida. It is this emotional and embodied *interaction* with the film that enables ethical investment, because the viewers can no longer forget about themselves in the film illusion. Given this haptic cinematic figuration chosen by Hanssen and his team, let us now take a closer look at the ethical dimension of *Ida's Diary*.

Taking artistic control over the pain of youth

In the 2010s, there has been an increased interest in the ethical consequences of producing and consuming film, with the emotional dimension of the cinematic experience being at the centre of the ethical inquiry. In an anthology on film ethics from 2014, Jinhee Choi and Mattias Frey point out that the viewer's perceptual and sensuous interaction gives a moral ground to relate to the world and people around, but it also is an ethical question in itself

(2014: 1). My close reading of the sequence where we see Ida self-harm for the first time reveals how the haptic quality of cinematography, sound design and editing triggers an embodied response to Ida's mental and physical pain. With the help of a complex repertoire of cinematic devices, Hanssen manages to mediate Ida's story without romanticizing or aestheticizing the violence that Ida uses against herself. The film makes it crystal clear that Ida is not an illusion or an abstraction and that her problems are acutely real and agonizing. Moreover, because the film does not show that which could or should not be shown, i.e. the way in which Ida self-harms, Hanssen avoids the feared social contagion that specialists warn about. This cinematic figuration aside, there are three other aspects of ethical nature that deserve attention: the role of the viewer as consumer of Ida's vulnerable intimacy, Ida's confidence in the camera and her confidence in Hanssen.

In an interview with the Norwegian magazine *A-magasinet*, Ida Storm explains that she started to film herself when she was seventeen and that the camera immediately became 'a trustworthy friend to whom I could tell everything'. In the beginning, the footage was not meant for publication, then Ida showed a clip to a friend, who encouraged her to do something with it: 'You have to use this, she said. I [Ida] don't dare, it was the first thing I thought'. Another factor that influenced Storm's decision to go public, were the rumours in her local community: 'People talked about the fact that Ida had been hospitalized. This bugged me [Ida] like hell. I wanted to show that I was not a model in a weekly magazine, not perfect, but this is who I am' (*A-magasinet* 2015: 8). On various occasions, like for example on Ida's blog on the film's official website, Ida explains how going public with her diagnosis and struggles was a tough, but also a rewarding and necessary process. She was contacted by people who had told her that the film had helped them to better understand what it was like to live with emotional unstable personality disorder and self-harm. Storm also used the film to front mental health as a subject in schools, which proves her social engagement. How is Storm's journey from pre- to post-production, from private footage to public talks, reflected in the film?

As already mentioned, in the film, we can see footage from the time before and after Ida contacted the production house Indie Film in 2009. More exactly, the first recordings used in the film are from 2006, while the last ones are from the summer of 2013. This means that Ida collaborated with Indie Film, and the film's director August B. Hanssen, for a period of five years. In the interview with *A-magasinet*, Storm mentions that the doctors were concerned about this collaboration: 'Will she endure it? How would others put up with it?' She also explains that she had moments when she doubted the film project. Nevertheless, it was important for her to continue, not least because she could set her own terms for the collaboration: no happy ending, no exposure of friends and family, no scenes that could trigger self-harm behaviour (*A-magasinet* 2015: 8–9). The final result, the film *Ida's Diary*, is evidence that Hanssen and his film team worked on Storm's terms. The film does not expose Storm's friends and family, whom we can see only on very rare occasions, and Storm's struggle against her own demons is not reduced to a cinematic cliché with a happy ending.

That said, it is questionable that the film does not give the viewers any prerequisites to reflect on how the film team worked together with Storm in the period from 2009 until the film release in 2014. In *Ida's Diary*, Ida appears alone and reassured in front of the camera, never in doubt about the film project that she initiated. This may explain why several reviewers oversaw the directorial control and described the film as a video diary rather than a creative treatment of it, a (self)mediation, as I have called this variant of first person cinema.

It is also difficult to see the viewers' role in the production of footage Ida delivers to Hanssen and Indie Film. Once Storm agrees to make a film together with Hanssen, she doesn't simply shoot for herself. For five years, she delivers raw material to a production house that will make a film based on her footage. And while Storm knows this because she signs a contract with Indie Film, the viewers remain unaware and therefore uncritical of their implicit role in the production and consumption of intimacy. This is particularly problematic when one considers that teenagers and young adults are the target audience of this film.

In the book *Disconnected: Youth, New Media, and the Ethics Gap*, the American sociologist Carrie James (2014) analyses the digital life of youth. James conducts extensive interviews with youth in the age group 10- to 25-years old and draws attention to what it means to grow up in an age where privacy is vulnerable and publicity can be used to make fun of, humiliate and punish another person. She finds out that many youths do not see and/or disconnect from the moral and ethical dimension of their actions and decisions on the Internet. James distinguishes between morality and ethics. If the first is an inclination to care about, show empathy to and engage with someone known or a small group, ethics is the capacity to think beyond the personal and the local, and figure what effects one's actions have on a larger, often more remote, community or society (James 2014: 5). In order to capture the ways in which youth disregard and disconnect from morality and ethics on the Internet, James introduces two terms: 'blind spots' and 'disconnects'. Where ethical blind spots are unconscious, naïve and unintentional, ethical disconnects imply that youth recognize the ethical and moral dimension in a situation; however, they choose to put it aside and instead favour more self-focused interests (James 2014: 10). In the book, James uses several disquieting examples from the United States about youth who post violating videos of each other on social media, which in turn leads to major stress and serious, sometimes even fatal, consequences.

Youth not only post videos of others, they also make videos of themselves at their happiest, but also at their most vulnerable. Storm is an example of how youth engage in practices of self-exposure. In *Ida's Diary*, Ida's trust in the camera seems unlimited. She sees the camera as a trustworthy friend she can always rely on and as an effective tool to control her difficult feelings and self-destructive behaviour. The film does little to increase youth's reflection about how the camera can become an infringing intruder and an instrument that can be used to hurt others and oneself. The liberating and healing aspect of the video diary is brought to the fore, while the vulnerability and ambivalence embedded in showing openly one's scars and problems is absent. Instead of doing something about the ethical blind spots and disconnects James talks about, the film sets them aside and becomes an (in)voluntary advocate that youth find themselves in front of the camera when they are at their most vulnerable.

Like the Norwegian psychologist and reality TV consultant Hedvig Montgomery (2016) remarks, this implies another ethical dilemma. In an online article in the Norwegian film magazine *Rushprint*, Montgomery writes:

> The producer and the broadcaster have an additional responsibility when young people and people who have just had difficult periods in their lives, tell stories. Their stories and self-image must be provided in ways that leave room for change. A 17-year-old may have a strong wish to talk about her self-harm, but this does not need to benefit her. It can be true without it being useful. The broadcaster must foresee that this young girl will want to stay for something else in only a few years, have other stories that mean more to her. One needs to make room for this more grown-up version of the participant, although she does not exist yet. It is the producer's responsibility to be ahead of her participants when it comes to understanding consequences.
>
> (2016)

Without mentioning *Ida's Diary*, yet with a clear reference to the film, Montgomery makes a call to hold the film professionals responsible for collaborations with young people who struggle. I have shown that Indie Film and Hanssen artistically treat Ida's unfiltered vulnerability and raw intimacy with respect and grace, yet it is more unclear whether the film makes room for a grown-up Ida Storm, as Montgomery calls for. In the contact ad in the film's prologue, Ida expresses her longing for a boyfriend, a wish that is repeated several times through the film, but the rest of the contact ad is by and large a diagnosis. This predilection to depict Ida's mental problems rather than her dreams for the future is at play in the rest of the film as well. On a few occasions, we do however hear how Ida hopes to get a normal adult life, with her family gathered around the dinner table. There seems to be a light at the end of the tunnel, although Hanssen, and Storm, did not want to make a film with a happy ending.

In the film's epilogue, Ida takes us on a hike to Galdhøpiggen, Norway's highest mountain. She is in close contact with nature and herself. The sky is blue and the landscape breathless and spectacular, with mountaintops still covered in snow projected against the blue summer sky. When Ida reaches the top of the mountain, she stretches out her arm and lets the camera she allegedly holds in her hand fly away. As the camera gains in altitude, a bird's-eye view reveals a little Ida surrounded by majestic mountaintops (Figure 7). The extradiegetic music underscores the hopeful atmosphere, but it is also worrying when the camera that Ida has held so close to her for so many years is transformed into a drone that watches her from above. Will the grown-up Ida Storm get to be more than the one who filmed her pain and showed her deep scars on the screen or will her intimate (self)mediation continue to hang above her for the rest of her life like a drone in the sky?

Figure 7: A bird's-eye view of Ida at the top of Norway's highest mountaintop, Galdhøpiggen. *Ida's Diary* (Hanssen, 2014). Cinematographers Karsten Heidar og Bob Aas Carho. 2014. Courtesy of Indie Film.

Conclusion

In this chapter, I have analysed the Norwegian film *Ida's Diary* as part of a culture in which more youth self-harm and where it has become increasingly common to share one's own vulnerability in front of the camera. I have proposed to treat the film as a first person film, although *Ida's Diary* does not comfortably fit conceptual dyads like explicitly versus implicitly autobiographical or fully autobiographical versus autobiographical in part. In *Ida's Diary*, Ida Storm films her own struggle against borderline disorder and self-harm at the same time that she delegates artistic control to a professional film team led by the director Hanssen at Indie Film. In order to capture the nature of this particular type of first person cinema, I have used the term (self)mediation. Through a close reading of the first self-harm occurring in the film, I have further shown how the film mobilizes haptic visuality, sound design and editing in order to make the viewers interact with Ida's pain and scars so that they can feel them on their own bodies rather than watching them from a distance. This sensuous interaction allows Storm to effectively front her case as a way to call for acceptance for youth who struggle with borderline personality and self-harm. It also enables the viewers to become ethically invested in Ida's story, and for this, the film must be praised. On the other hand, there are other more problematic aspects embedded in Ida's (self)mediation. The film conceals the fact that Ida Storm had a close collaboration with Hanssen in the period 2009 to 2013, when she kept a video diary not only for herself, but also for what eventually became *Ida's Diary*. I have argued that this concealment blocks the viewer's capacity to critically reflect on her own role in the production and consumption of pain. Also, *Ida's Diary* does not reflect on the camera's ambivalent role in relation to the exposure Hanssen and Storm initiated. The camera is not merely a friend and supporter, it can quickly become an intruder and a burden. This throws off the ethical balance also in an otherwise ethically robust film like *Ida's Diary*.

Notes

1 This and all the following translations from the Norwegian media are mine.
2 This and all the following translations from the film are mine.
3 A jump cut is an editing technique used in film whereby almost identical shots are edited together in a sequence, creating the visual effect that the image 'jumps'.

Chapter 5

Reclaiming Sami identity: Of blood and genes

Northern Sweden in the 1930s: three official visitors from Uppsala arrive at a small boarding school for indigenous Sami children. The children are lined up in front of the school and they all wear *kofte*, the traditional Sami garment. At the teacher's instruction, the 14-year-old Elle-Marja (Lena Cecilia Sparrok) takes a few steps forward and presents the visitors a traditional Sami gift made of reindeer antlers. After a quick inspection of the children's clothes and looks, the girls are separated from the boys and moved inside the school in line formation, with Elle-Marja leading the group. Once in the classroom, Elle-Marja is asked to take off her *kofte* and sit on a chair by the teacher's desk. One of the two male visitors, a young scientist, inspects her teeth and skin colour, and takes measurements of her skull and nose (Figure 8). The camera focuses close-ups and extreme close-ups of Elle-Marja, who asks twice the scientist in bewilderment what he is doing. The scientist chooses to neglect the Sami girl and instead directs all his questions and instructions to the teacher in third person, as if Elle-Marja is not a worthy partner of conversation: 'Are both *her* parents of Sami origin?', 'Now, *she* can go there and take off *her* clothes,' 'Does *she*

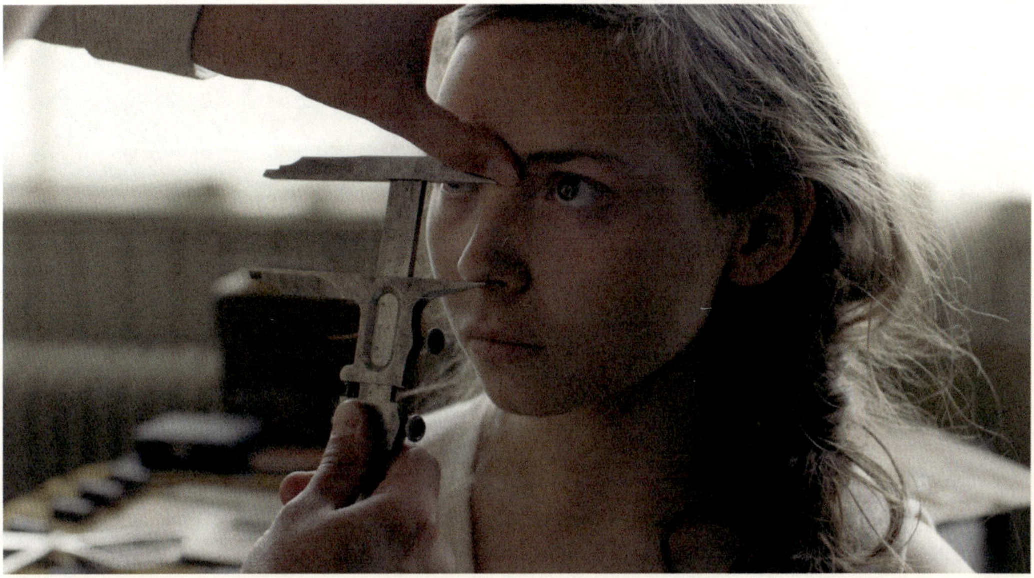

Figure 8: A Swedish scientist measures Elle-Marja (Lena Cecilia Sparrok)'s nose. *Sami Blood* (Kernell, 2016). Cinematographer Sophia Olsson. 2016. Courtesy of Nordisk Film Production AB.

understand?' (emphasis added). From the side, the teacher confirms Elle-Marja's Sami background and overlooks the procedures, seconding the scientist's instructions and making sure Elle-Marja obeys his orders. 'Elle-Marja, be a good example', she says in a strict tone, when the Sami girl hesitates to take off the rest of her clothes and pose naked in front of the camera mounted on a tripod in the middle of the classroom. Through two point-of-view (POV) shots from Elle-Marja's perspective, we see how several local boys oversee the procedures by peeping through the opened classroom window. The POVs together with the close-ups and extreme close-ups make the viewer inhabit Elle-Marja's pain and humiliation at being treated as an interesting 'specimen' rather than a human being of same worth as the Swedes. 'Elle-Marja!', the teacher commands, as the Sami girl finally undresses and the scientist forces her to hold her arms behind her head. The camera films Elle-Marja from behind, with the focus on the back of her head and her naked shoulders, while in the background we distinguish the blurry silhouettes of the rest of the girls (Figure 9). Every time the scientist's camera secures yet another picture of the naked Elle-Marja, the flash of the camera and the sound of the blitz are dramatically enhanced so as to underline this incredibly invasive moment. When the visitors finish their photography session with Elle-Marja, they move on to measuring and photographing the other girls.

In the next scene, the camera follows Elle-Marja outside the school in handheld. Instrumental music is added to the soundtrack to underline Elle-Marja's pain and embarrassment. When Elle-Marja passes by the group of boys who peeped through the classroom window, one of them tells his mates 'See, there comes the circus animal' and adds:

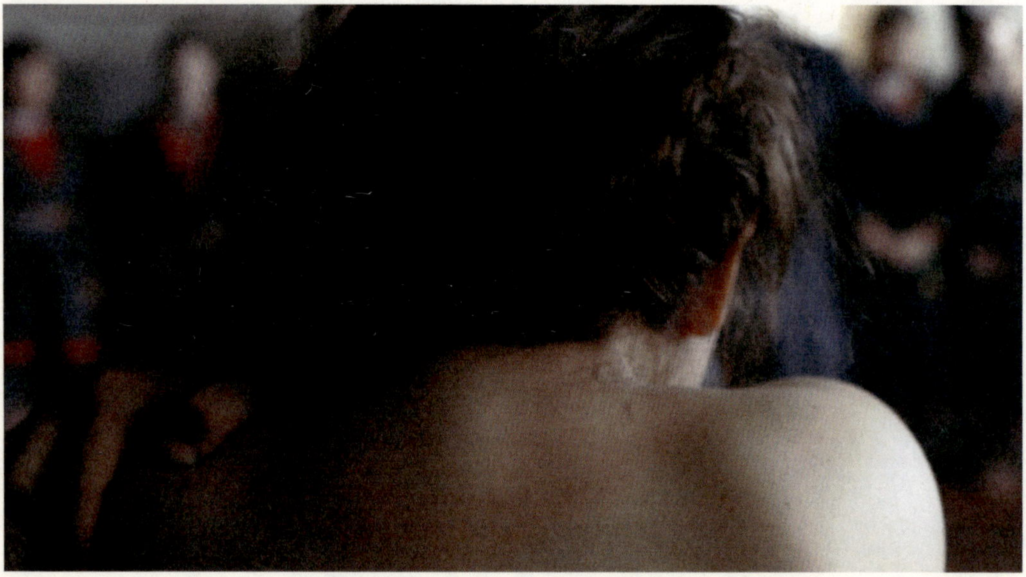

Figure 9: Elle-Marja (Lena Cecilia Sparrok) is forced to pose naked in front of the scientists' camera. *Sami Blood* (Kernell, 2016). Cinematographer Sophia Olsson. 2016. Courtesy of Nordisk Film Production AB.

'They [the Sami] are on a lower stage of development. That's why they look like this', echoing the scientific discourse of the time. Irritated and upset, Elle-Marja confronts him and asks him to take his words back. She also threatens him with her Sami knife, yet the boys quickly immobilize her. They push her down to the ground, hold her head tight as the offender chops off a piece of her ear in a similar fashion to how Elle-Marja earmarked a reindeer calf in a previous scene. The camera cross-cuts from medium close-ups of the attacker filmed from below to medium close-ups of Elle-Marja lying on the ground, which suggests the power imbalance both in terms of physical might and social hierarchy. The ravaging shame of having to pose naked in front of Swedish scientists and random voyeurs is now doubled up by the shame of being literally earmarked as a 'circus animal'. And all because of Elle-Marja's Sami background.

These incredibly demeaning scenes are taken from Amanda Kernell's critically acclaimed feature *Sameblod* (*Sami Blood*) (2016). *Sami Blood* is Kernell's brilliant attempt to fictionalize the racism and abuse experienced by the indigenous Sami at the hands of the Nordic majorities (Kvist 1994; Minde 2005). The protagonist in *Sami Blood*, Elle-Marja, turns her back to her Sami community and embraces all things Swedish in an attempt to wipe out her Sami identity. Her way to deal with racism is to disconnect, while her younger sister Njenna (Mia Erika Sparrok) chooses to stay and continue the traditional livelihood of reindeer husbandry. Elle-Marja's story of disconnect is not an exception. Just like her, many Sami moved away from their families, stopped speaking Sami and distanced themselves from everything associated with the Sami culture. As a result, generations of children have grown up with little or no knowledge of their Sami heritage.

In this chapter, I propose the closer investigation of two Norwegian first person films in which the directors use the camera to recover and reconnect with their lost Sami identity: Ellen-Astri Lundby's *Min mors hemmelighet* (*Suddenly Sami*) (2009) and Yvonne Thomassen's *Familiebildet* (*My Family Portrait*) (2013). Both films have been partly financed by the Norwegian Film Institute (Lundby 2017; Nermoen 2017). Neither *Suddenly Sami* nor *My Family Portrait* had an ordinary cinema distribution in Norway. Instead, the films reached audiences through broadcasting, international film festivals and other alternative cinema circuits. *Suddenly Sami* was shown on TV2, Norway's largest commercial television broadcaster, for an estimated audience of 434,000 viewers after three viewings in 2009 (Lundby 2018). *My Family Portrait* was shown on the Norwegian public broadcaster NRK 2 and reached 323,000 viewers in nine viewings spread across three years, from 2014 to 2016 (Thomassen 2018a). In addition, thousands of Norwegian pupils in secondary school saw both films through Den kulturelle skolesekken (The Cultural Schoolbag), which is a state-funded programme meant to familiarize Norwegian pupils with various forms of contemporary culture and make them aware of culture's role in society.

Both films also participated in the international film festival circuit, reaching audiences wide and far. *Suddenly Sami* has had a very productive and unusually long festival life. The film has been shown at more than twenty film festivals around the world, many of which have an indigenous profile like the Taiwan International Aboriginal Film Festival or the Native Spirit Festival in London. In fact, the film continued to be solicited by festival organizers around the world several years after its official release in Norway (Lundby 2017). It also toured Guatemala at the initiative of the Norwegian Ministry of Foreign Affairs on two different occasions, in 2010 and 2011, and the film's DVD was distributed to all the Norwegian Embassies and Consulates abroad (Lundby 2018).

My Family Portrait participated in 22 festivals in Norway and abroad and received three important distinctions: the Debut Prize Skårungen at Tromsø International Film Festival in 2013, the Public's Award at the 2013 Eurodok and an Honourable Mention at the 2013 International Film Festival for Environment, Health, and Culture in Jakarta (Thomassen 2018b). Last, but not least, both films can be streamed through platforms connected to the public library system in Norway like filmrommet.no, FilmBiB and filmarkivet.no.

If Kernell mobilizes fiction to reconstruct and explain how and why some Sami could have disconnected from their cultural heritage, Lundby and Thomassen use the first person mode of address to show their own entangled road back to a lost Sami identity. It is particularly intriguing to look at *Suddenly Sami* and *My Family Portrait* through the lens of *Sami Blood*. The histories of racism against the Sami are similar in Norway and Sweden, although Kernell's film remains rooted in the Swedish realities of the 1930s. In the scenes from *Sami Blood* in which the Swedish scientists measure the Sami children, it becomes particularly clear how biology was put in the service of a racist ideology that legitimized the discrimination of the Sami as an inferior race. This racist mentality permeated the scientific community, the school and the Swedish society at large, with Swedish officials like Elle-Marja's teacher commonly projecting vulnerability onto the Sami communities in an attempt to 'civilize', i.e. contain them. As Lundby and Thomassen embark on a personal journey to recuperate a lost Sami identity in the 2000s, biology makes a surprising comeback. Met by the silence of their mothers and grandmothers, both directors turn to biology and genetics as discursive resources in reconnecting with their Sami roots. In this chapter, I discuss the paradoxes of this return to biology through a close reading of specific scenes from the films and by showing how the legacy of racism continues to permeate contemporary struggles over what it means to be Sami.

'We are all 100 per cent'

Suddenly Sami and *My Family Portrait* are not simply idiosyncratic, although in both films, directors focus on their own family histories. Like *Sami Blood*, these first person films are actively engaged in the contemporary sociopolitical and cultural struggles about what it means to be Sami in the 2000s. In the 2000s, Sami identity, or Saminess, has been the subject of much debate and contestation not only in relation to the Nordic majorities, but also within the Sami communities themselves. In Sweden and Finland, the status of being a Sami is strictly connected to membership in the Sami electoral register (Lindi 2017; Berg-Nordlie and Skogvang 2016). This has led to rigorous scrutiny of the criteria for membership in the electoral roll, particularly in Finland where a fraction of self-declared Sami made their own organization after being denied membership in the Finnish Sami electoral roll (Lindi 2017; Berg-Nordlie and Skogvang 2016).

Unlike in Sweden and Finland, in Norway, those who do not or cannot register in the Sami electoral roll, but consider themselves Sami, are also entitled to draw affiliation to Saminess (Lindi 2017; Berg-Nordlie and Skogvang 2016). This liberal approach does not mean that the question of who is a Sami is undisputed. On the Sami's national day on 6 February 2017, Rolf Rødven wrote a post on his Facebook wall and started a debate that demonstrates the contested nature of Saminess in Norway in the 2000s. The ingrained shame that many generations of Sami grew up with once again came to the surface, this time not so much as a story of disconnect, as exemplified through Elle-Marja's story in *Sami Blood*, but as a confession of difficult connect to Saminess and a call for an inclusive Sami pride.

In his Facebook post, Rødven took issue with denominations that graded one's Sami identity according to measures such as 'full', 'half' and 'quarter' Sami (Lindi 2017). Rødven's post spread quickly through social media and it also got the attention of the Norwegian public broadcaster NRK, who interviewed Rødven as well as other public figures of Sami origin about their position vis-à-vis the use of fractions to denominate Saminess. In the NRK article, Rødven talks about the dilemma of having to relate to Sami fractions in a northern Norwegian context that has been multicultural for hundreds of years. Instead of pitching one cultural identity against the other by classifying people according to fractions, Rødven calls for Sami pride to unite his community. He references in agreement a conversation he had with the Sami actress Ebba Joks: 'As Ebba so great said it to me: "You cannot be one quarter Sami. Which part of you is then Sami? Where is your Sami 'I' located, up or down, right or left? We are all 100 per cent"' (Lindi 2017).[1]

In the article, NRK also quotes one of the comments to Rødven's post that witnesses similar experiences to Rødven's, in particular in conversations with ethnic Norwegians: 'I often get questions whether I am "completely Sami", most often from Norwegians, perhaps because I do not quite fit into the stereotype of how a Sami should look like. I guess few Norwegians get their genes so carefully scrutinized all the time' (Lindi 2017). Interviewed by the NRK, the young politician Christina Henriksen from the National Association of Norwegian Sami (NSR) argues that it is primarily the Sami themselves who categorize each other according to fractions: 'I know that many call themselves half, quarter or eighth Sami. I have nothing to spare for such designations, but I think it is largely us who use the definitions'. Also the Norwegian Labour Party politician Helga Pedersen tells the NRK that she understands Rødven's dilemma. Pedersen found her Sami origins carefully examined by her own when she was listed as candidate for the Sami Parliament in Norway in 2016 (Pedersen 2016). In response to Rødven's post, Pedersen says: 'To be referred to as partly Sami sounds less well than to be a full blood Sami. It is a choice of words that contributes to exclusion and alienation from Saminess' (Lindi 2017).

The debate initiated by Rødven is interesting not only because it points to some of the tensions within the Sami community in the 2010s, but also because it illustrates how the fraction mentality becomes a contemporary spin-off from the racist ideology that made Sami children like Elle-Marja valuable objects of scientific research. In the 1930s, Elle-Marja was seen as a 'circus animal', a pure Sami specimen well adapted to living conditions in the arctic nature and climate, but not made to survive life in the city, as the teacher explains when Elle-Marja informs her she wants to study in Uppsala. If Elle-Marja's allegedly 100 per cent Sami background became a problem for her in the 1930s, in the late 2010s Rødven and others like him are weary of describing their background in fractions that suggest that they are anything less than 100 per cent Sami.

The fraction debate is one example of the internal struggles over Saminess that shape a new generation of Sami in search of their Sami identity. The short mockumentary *Skabmagovat* (*Colonial Gaze Sami Artists' Collective*) (2012) co-directed by Sami filmmakers Elle-Máijá Tailfeathers and Marja Bål Nango is another pointed remark in that sense. In the film, we meet a collective of Sami artists who struggle to draft a manifesto that can unite their artistic enterprise under the common denominator 'Sami art'. According to film scholars Scott Mackenzie and Anna W. Stenport, *Colonial Gaze Sami Artists' Collective* 'provides a tongue-in-cheek commentary to dominant strands of Sami documentary filmmaking' that rely on activist, realist and revivalist discourses (Mackenzie and Stenport 2016: 179). As it does that, the film also pokes fun at the debates surrounding the question of Sami identity in the 2010s. After sipping from a bottle of Russian vodka, the leader of the collective, Matti Aikio, reveals that he has Polish and not Sami origins as the rest of the collective initially thought. This unexpected confession prompts the collective to discuss the question of who is a Sami. Some voices around the table do not think that it is possible to become a Sami. 'I don't want to offend anyone but for me becoming Sami all of a sudden is a very strange thought', says the collective's vice-president. 'Yeah, it's not possible', says another. Aikio fumbles to dismiss this by defining Saminess as a culture into which one can grow: 'And, like, there is no, there is no … You cannot. There is not a genetic Sami. There is not a biological Sami. Or non-Sami. It's impossible to define', he says hesitantly and adds: 'It's more a cultural, it's a cultural definition. But what is a cultural definition? That's even more difficult to define'.

Unlike *Colonial Gaze Sami Artists' Collective*, Ellen-Astri Lundby's *Suddenly Sami* and Yvonne Thomassen's *My Family Portrait* do not afford a parodic-ironic treatment of the questions of who can be and how to become a Sami. In both films, we see the directors developing their own Sami identity in real time so to speak. As they shoot, both Lundby and Thomassen find out that they have Sami origins. This is affectively and intellectually demanding not least since filming is an inherent part of the process. Major questions arise and unfold. Why have their families kept their Sami origins hidden and how does one assume a newly discovered Sami identity? It is particularly the second question that I want to address in the following discussion.

'Look at your high cheekbones!'

In *My Family Portrait*, the director Yvonne Thomassen tries to gather her mother and her five siblings to take a last family photograph together with their 90-year-old mother, Thomassen's grandmother. Starting from a family portrait taken in studio years before her grandfather passed away (Figure 10), Thomassen embarks on making a first person film that proves to be much more challenging than initially anticipated. As it turns out, the six siblings no longer wish to keep in touch with each other after what they describe as a difficult and split childhood. They see their mother as having an important role in the family split and blame her for cultivating a culture of silence rather than open dialog when they grew up. In the first part of the film, this silence is explained as an attempt to put behind traumatic experiences during the Second World War when the family was forced to evacuate their home in Lerresfjord as the Nazi troops engaged in scorched-earth war tactics. In the second half of the film, the film narrative takes a sudden shift, and a new layer of silence is shown to split Thomassen's family.

Personal black-and-white photographs in her grandmother's family album turn out to play a central role in the disclosure incited by Thomassen's film project. In voice-over, against a montage of photographs of Thomassen's grandfather helping reindeer-herding Sami to move their herds across the fjord, Thomassen shares how she accidentally found out about her Sea Sami origins. The camera cuts smoothly from one picture to another, slightly zooming in and out of each picture and slowly panning from left to right and right to left in an attempt to animate the old stills. Thomassen's commentary in voice-over is accompanied by extradiegetic string music softly marking the slow editing pace. The director

Figure 10: The old family photograph taken in studio and depicting Thomassen's grandparents and their six children. *My Family Portrait* (Thomassen, 2013). Cinematographer Olaug Spissøy Kyvik. 2013. Courtesy of Yvonne Thomassen.

explains how her mother revealed in a brief commentary to these pictures that Thomassen's grandfather spoke Sami and that both he and Thomassen's grandmother were Sea Sami. After showing the black-and-white photographs from her grandmother's album, the camera cuts to an archival picture in the Sophus Tromholt Collection taken in the beginning of the 1880s. This is the last photograph in the montage and depicts a group of Sea Sami in traditional clothing looking straight into the camera. Inscribed in the World Heritage List of the United Nations Educational, Scientific and Cultural Organization (UNESCO), the Sophus Tromholt Collection is considered to be a unique record of the indigenous Sami that eschews racially charged depictions characteristic of the time (UNESCO 2013). As the camera focuses on this picture, the director describes how her mother's revelation took her completely by surprise, not least because she grew up with negative stereotypes about the Sami and learned to use the word 'Sami' as an ethnic slur. This comment, corroborated with the visual shift from silenced family photographs to celebrated archival material, subtly suggests the national dimension of this demeaning narrative, which the Sea Sami eventually came to internalize. Then, Thomassen continues in voice-over that it took her an entire year to dare to ask her grandmother about their Sami roots, a conversation that she reveals in the scene immediately following the montage of old photographs.

We are in her grandmother's kitchen and her grandmother's brother Hagbart is visiting. In an establishing long shot, we see Thomassen sitting by the table in the left corner of the screen and her grandmother and her brother sitting across the table from her. They have three cups of coffee in front of them. In voice-over, Thomassen explains that she had never met her granduncle before, which convinces her even more that the time was ripe to finally ask her grandmother about their Sami origin. As the camera cuts back and forth from long shots of the two siblings sitting by the table to close-ups of particularly her grandmother's face, but also Hagbart's, we hear Thomassen speaking off-screen.

YVONNE: Do you have Sami blood?
HAGBART: Sami blood, well, if one comes originally from … in other words, this has something to do with genes.
YVONNE: I didn't know that we had Sami ancestry.
HAGBART: No, well … yeah …
YVONNE: You have not told me about this [*takes a short break as the camera focuses a close-up of her grandmother*] Do you have enough Sami in you that you could have worn a *kofte*?
GRANDMOTHER: I don't know [*laughs nervously*]. Who can know that? We cannot measure the blood whether it is Sami or Norwegian or [*grandmother takes a short break, Hagbart mumbles undistinguishable words in the background*] for the blood is the same, I think.

In this scene, we see Thomassen's first attempts to assume her Sami identity by asking her grandmother and her brother to confirm their Sami ancestry. She defines Saminess by blood and describes it as an interiority that in turn can legitimize the wearing of the traditional Sami garment *kofte*. In reaction, her granduncle fumbles and avoids, unable to finish his sentences, while Thomassen's grandmother says she does not know whether she is Sami or not. She also dismisses a definition of Saminess by blood. The close shots of the two elderly faces reveal distress, a controlled panic of sorts suggestively communicated through the exchange of glances.

This short scene foreshadows other conversations Thomassen will have with her mother, her aunt Hallfrid and her grandmother later in the film. During these conversations, histories of discrimination and abuse become evident. For example, Norwegian authorities banned the Sami language in schools, and after the Second World War, speaking Sami was seen as unpatriotic, which made many parents stop speaking Sami to their children also at home. Or, it was more shameful to be a Sea Sami than a Mountain Sami, a shame also sustained by internal hierarchies within the Sami community. In these conversations, Thomassen, her aunt and her mother talk about a culture that has been taken away from them once the Sami language disappeared.

In the present, Saminess is systematically framed as interiority, something that resides inside you, placed in the blood and revealed by phenotypic traits like high cheekbones. For example, when Thomassen asks her aunt why she was never told about her Sami background, the aunt replies: 'Look at your high cheekbones! Look at yourself in the mirror and you'll see there is a Sami in you also in some other places'. This shows how biological discourses are mobilized to define Saminess. Wearing the traditional Sami garment *kofte* is a way to live out what is written in the blood. That is why getting a *kofte* is so important for Thomassen. Her mother decides to sew one for her, and the first time she puts it on, we see Thomassen overwhelmed by emotions. Yet, before she can wear the *kofte* with pride, she seeks a final confirmation from her grandmother.

Four years have passed since Thomassen first found out about her Sami origins and we are back in her grandmother's kitchen. Like three years ago, the two women representing two generations sit across from each other by the kitchen table with a cup of coffee in front of them. Speaking on-screen, Thomassen opens by explaining her decision to owe a *kofte* and asks her grandmother once again about their Sami origins. As the conversation develops, close-ups of Thomassen and her grandmother are symbolically edited together to suggest tight family bonds, but also generational differences. When the grandmother asserts with certainty that she is not of Sami ancestry, Thomassen pulls out her grandmother's genealogical tree made by one of her cousins (Figure 11). The tree attests that her grandmother's great grandfather on her mother's side was a Sea Finn, which is the old denomination for Sea Sami.

YVONNE: So we have a little bit of Sea Finn inside.
GRANDMOTHER: Yes, yes, then it must be like this. That's why we are short. [*Thomassen starts to laugh and so does her grandmother*]
YVONNE: Yes, that's why we have high cheekbones.
GRANDMOTHER: Yeah.

YVONNE: So this makes me fully entitled to wear a *kofte*.
GRANDMOTHER: Of course, and so is everyone else in the Norwegian country, the majority, in any case up here [in northern Norway].

The conversation ends with Thomassen trying to figure out why their Sami ancestry has been kept hidden from her, an explanation she only partly procures from her grandmother. After reiterating the difference between Sea and Mountain Sami and expressing her bewilderment at the Sea Sami's unwillingness to talk about their origins, the grandmother concludes: 'People are people. What matters is how they behave, I have said this before, irrespective of where they come from'. Indirectly, the grandmother suggests that the internal hierarchies among the Sea and Mountain Sami have contributed to why many Sea Sami have kept hidden their Sami origins.

It is strong, moving, but also disquieting to see how Thomassen assumes Saminess in front of her grandmother in the 2010s. She mobilizes biological discourses of blood and phenotypic traits to recuperate a culture that has been taken away from her. For when all cultural traces are lost, the body becomes the place in which to look for Saminess. Seen from a historical perspective, this presents us with a cruel paradox.

At the turn of the twentieth century, Norwegian authorities were not only keen to assimilate the Sami linguistically and culturally through the policy of Norwegianization. Norwegian scientists, just like the Swedish scientists depicted in *Sami Blood*, were also eagerly engaged in measuring Sami bodies, including skulls and bones, in an attempt to isolate

Figure 11: Yvonne reads out loud the genealogy tree to her grandmother. *My Family Portrait* (Thomassen, 2013). Cinematographer Olaug Spissøy Kyvik. 2013. Courtesy of Yvonne Thomassen.

the biological and behavioural aspects of the Sami population. As physical anthropology became an established academic field at the University of Oslo, and Sami skulls gained a high scientific value, scientists worked diligently to define a pool of Sami phenotypic traits based on measurements of cephalic index, body height, eye and hair colour, to name a few.

In a study of physical anthropology in Norway in the period 1890–1945, Norwegian historian Jon R. Kyllingstad shows how the notion of Sami primitiveness as racially determined permeated the research of several Norwegian scientists at the time. On the one hand, Kyllingstad lists the extreme voices like the Norwegian geologist and ethnographer Andreas Martin Hansen (1857–1932). Based on measurements of human relics, Hansen challenged the status of the Sami as first-comers in Scandinavia. He developed a racial hierarchy with the long-skulled Aryans at the top and the 'dwarf-like' Sami at the bottom, and advanced a theory that the Sea Sami were racially different from the reindeer-herding Sami, placing the Sea Sami above the Mountain Sami in his racial hierarchy, yet below the Aryans (Kyllingstad 2014: 79–81). As Kyllingstad underlines, Hansen did not win general scientific acclaim, but his theories led to much public debate, influencing public opinion and impacting later research such as Halfdan Bryn's politically charged work on the racial composition of Troms (2014: 121–22). It is also striking to note how *My Family Portrait* attests to internal hierarchies within the Sami communities that unpleasantly resonate with Hansen's racial hierarchy. Consequently, if Hansen saw the Sea Sami as 'more developed' than the Mountain Sami, Thomassen's family speaks of a reversed situation within the Sami community: the Sea Sami felt a deep shame of being less Sami than the Mountain Sami.

Unlike Hansen, other Norwegian scientists at the time were more moderate in relation to the question of racial determinism. Here, Kyllingstad points attention to Kristian Emil Schreiner and his wife Alette, who played a major role in the establishment of physical anthropology as a field of research at the University of Oslo. Unlike their colleague Halfdan Bryn, who actively promoted eugenic measures to prevent the 'bastardization' of the Nordic race, the Schreiners had a less deterministic view of race and biology, dismissing the idea of a Nordic Master race and speaking positively about genetic variation (Kyllingstad 2014: 156). Yet, in their studies of the anthropology of the Sami, it becomes clear that the idea of racial hierarchies influenced much of their work. They both operated with the notion of Sami primitiveness, which they traced in bodily appearance, but also in psychology. Kristian Emil Schreiner identified a pool of 'Mongol-like' bodily characteristics in the Sami such as low stature and poor beard growth, and which, according to him, implied that the Sami belonged to a primitive race (Kyllingstad 2014: 147). His wife, Alette, further tied these bodily characteristics to psychology, describing the Sami as infantile, carefree, cheerful, shy and simpleminded (Kyllingstad 2012: 54; 2014: 147).

If Alette Schreiner portrayed the 'primitive' Sami in contradictory manners, backward and stagnant, yet perfectly adapted to the environment and living harmonious lives in contact with nature (Kyllingstad 2014: 156), in the folk censuses from the interwar period, the positive notions of harmony and perfect adaptation were long gone. According to cultural historian Bente Persen, as late as 1950, Norway Statistics classified the Sami as 'deviants' in the same category with the blind, the deaf, the mentally disabled and the insane (Persen 2008: 74).

This shows how a few decades after being scientifically measured, psychologized and racialized, the Sami body was ripe to be medicalized and even psychiatricized. Reframed as a question of vulnerability, the notion of Sami primitiveness allowed Norwegian authorities, such as teachers and priests, to take upon themselves the task to 'civilize' the Sami by wiping out their language and traditions. That is why it is a cruel paradox that Thomassen looks for Saminess where Norwegian (and Swedish) scientists strove so hard to place it, namely in the body. A nonagenarian, Thomassen's grandmother is old enough to remember the biopolitics that constructed the Sami body as 'primitive' and 'deviant'. Her defensive answer when first confronted about her Sami origins ('You cannot measure the blood if it is Sami or Norwegian', she says) must therefore be understood in the light of the scientific discourse that tied Saminess first to biology and, then via biology, to notions of racial determinism and social Darwinism. Four years later, when Thomassen pulls out her family's genealogical tree, the grandmother finally accepts her Sami origins. She does that not only in front of her granddaughter, but also in front of the camera and by extension in front of national and international audiences. Although she now manages to chuckle at the racialization of phenotypic traits like short bodies and high cheekbones together with her granddaughter, she is also quick to underline that it is how people behave what matters, and not how they look.

See your results: Haplogroup V

If Thomassen uses an old-school genealogical tree to obtain her grandmother's confirmation, Ellen-Astri Lundby mobilizes other resources in the process of developing her Sami identity in *Suddenly Sami*. In the film, we see Lundby's mother sick with Alzheimer's disease, a condition that has impacted significantly also her language capabilities (Figure 12). The film implies that a long-suppressed language came to the surface when the director's mother withdrew from family and society into herself. This language attests to the mother's Sea Sami origins, an identity that she had also kept hidden from her daughter. Perhaps one of the most suggestive scenes in this sense is when Lundby plays a Sea Sami joik for her mother and the latter responds by humming along and shaking her head, a reaction that contradicts the apathetic mood into which Lundy's mother otherwise dwells.

Because of her mother's declining health, Lundby is however unable to engage her in a discussion about her Sami origins like Thomassen does with her grandmother. Instead, she seeks answers from her mother's relatives in Lerresfjord (the same place Thomassen has her family roots from) and from bureaucrats at the Sami Parliament in Karasjok. She also re-enacts scenes from her childhood in an attempt to resurrect the past and recover the truth that has been hidden from her (Figure 13). Just like Thomassen in *My Family Portrait*, she mixes her own recordings with official archival material (film clips and photographs) and personal archives (mainly family photographs, but also a film clip) to underline the interplay between

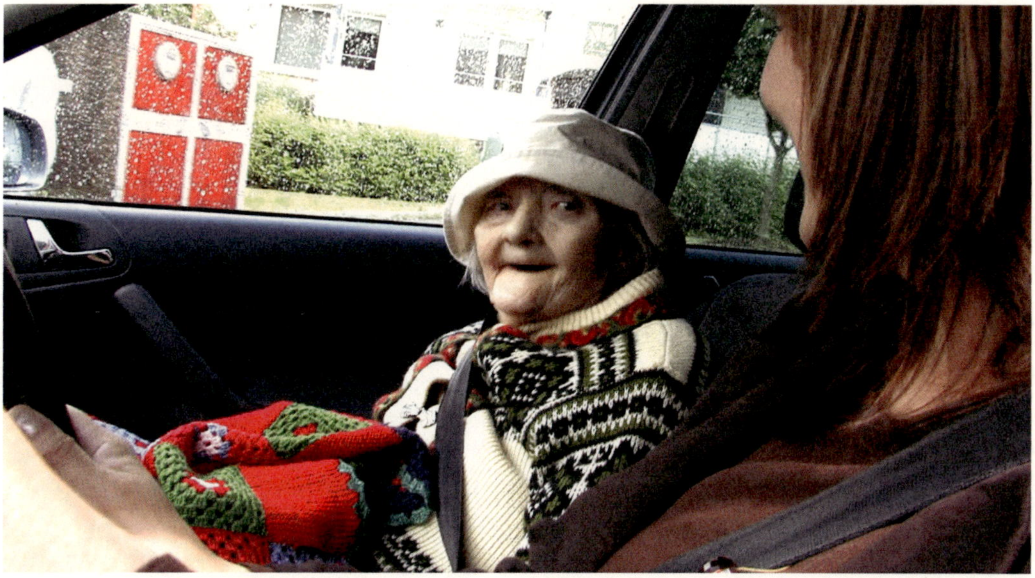

Figure 12: Ellen-Astri Lundby driving her mother. *Suddenly Sami* (Lundby, 2009). Cinematographer Runar Jarle Wiik. 2009. Courtesy of Ellen-Astri Lundby.

Figure 13: A reenacted scene of a childhood memory in which Ellen-Astri remembers receiving a Sami hat from her grandmother in northern Norway. *Suddenly Sami* (Lundby, 2009). Cinematographer Runar Jarle Wiik. 2009. Courtesy of Ellen-Astri Lundby.

her personal story and the fate of the Sami community in a national perspective. Suggestively, in the first official archival clip used in the film, Lundby is even able to spot herself as a 9-year-old young girl marching in front of the royal palace in Oslo on the occasion of the Norwegian Constitution Day. A family photograph of her and her mother taken on the same day follows this official clip borrowed from the Norwegian public broadcaster NRK. The visual rhetoric in this personal photograph is very much in tandem with the film clip from the NRK: mother and daughter are festively dressed, both smiling and posing in front of the Oslo City Council as a Norwegian flag waves from a boat in the left corner of the picture. In retrospect, this montage of official and personal records underlines that the official national pride of being Norwegian did not room a Sami identity in the late 1960s.

Also like in *My Family Portrait*, the mother's unwillingness to talk about her Sami origins is tied to histories of discrimination and abuse at the hands of the Norwegian authorities as well as to the collective shame the indigenous Sami came to internalize as a consequence of such discriminatory practices. The Second World War is seen to have acerbated the shame to be a Sami, a shame Lundby's mother successfully camouflaged by 'becom[ing] Norwegian the moment she left northern Norway', to quote her brother in Lerresfjord. At the end of the war, Lundby's mother moved to Oslo, leaving behind not only a community devastated by the war, but also her family, her mother tongue and her Sami identity. In Oslo, she made a new family, married an ethnically Norwegian man, had a girl, Ellen-Astri, moved to a new apartment in the suburbs, and enjoyed modern life in the city. Like Elle-Marja in *Sami Blood*, Lundby's mother chose to disconnect, keeping only seldom contact with her family in northern Norway.

In order to illustrate visually how common the Sami disconnect was, Lundy includes a model of the folk census from Kvænangen Municipality in northern Norway, which is the neighbouring municipality to where Lundby's mother comes from. The model consists of small wooden figurines that hold up posters indicating their ethnic affiliation: the ethnic Norwegians hold a Norwegian flag, the Sami and the Kvens (an ethnic minority who emigrated into Norway from the northern parts of Finland) hold white posters on which their ethnicity is displayed in black capital letters. If in 1930, close to a half of the figurines carried Sami and Kven-posters, twenty years later, in 1950, the number of Norwegian flags increased drastically, with only one Sami and one Kven figurine left. This suggests how not only those who left, but also those who stayed in the area chose to officially shed their Saminess by declaring themselves Norwegian in the folk census.

While shooting *Suddenly Sami*, Lundby regains contact not only with her relatives, whom she visits on several occasions. More importantly, she assumes a racialized identity that her mother tried to 'protect' her from when she turned her back to Saminess and started a new life in Oslo. If Lundby's relatives in Lerresfjord have different strategies to assume their Sami identity (for example, her uncle is an official member of the Sami electoral register), Lundby feels she needs more time before she can take the official step of registering in the Sami electoral roll. Instead, she seeks a confirmation of her Sami roots in genetics.

Five minutes in the film, and before she heads to northern Norway, we see her sending a saliva sample to the Genographic Project initiated by the National Geographic Society. As she opens the package from the Genographic Project, she finds a CD-ROM that she then plays on her computer. The camera films the computer screen as Lundby clicks on the introductory video. The video opens with the following white-on-black text being typed on the screen against a soundtrack of computer-simulated metallic sounds punctuated by the sound of typing: 'Your DNA contains the greatest history book ever written'. Genetics thus proudly promise to deliver greater historical insight than any historical annals. As the video starts to roll, the camera cuts back and forth between the computer screen, showing fast-edited close-ups of mostly men belonging to different ethnicities, and close-ups of Lundby, who watches the video in deep fascination. The male voice-of-authority on the video announces in English:

> You may have your mother's smile or your father's hair. But why do you look the way you do? How do you explain the incredible diversity of people around the globe and how did your ancestors find their way to the place where you live today?

Lundby then transfers to the bathroom where we see her taking her saliva sample. Halfway through the film, she finally gets her results. She is once again in front of her computer, with the camera cutting back and forth between shots of the computer screen and close-ups of Lundby. As Lundy clicks on the tab 'SEE YOUR RESULTS', we see her face in bewilderment: 'I don't understand a thing. I have ended up in Spain. This doesn't make sense. What?', she says. A new shot of the computer screen shows what Lundby reacts to: Lundby's genetic material is visualized as a cartographic image in which we see twenty dots spread across three continents and a red line that starts in Africa and ends in Southern Europe. As she moves with her mouse along the red line, she remarks that one dot is placed in northern Norway. When she clicks on it, a new text box opens with 'Saami culture' written on it. Lundy then proceeds to read out loud an excerpt from the report sent by the Genographic Project, which states that her haplogroup is Vee as in Victor, and not five as she mistakenly reads out. Because haplogroup V attains its highest concentration among the Skolt Sami of northern Scandinavia, Lundby can happily conclude that she has genetic proof of her Sami ancestry.

As Lundby strives to make sense of her genetic results, one cannot help to remark the difficult language of genetics that attests to the complexity of the human genome pinpointing among others the migration histories of a person's ancestors. Encoded in the annals of her DNA, 'the greatest book of history ever written' turns out to be too convoluted in the scientific jargon. So why resort to this incomprehensible language, which indeed decodes her DNA, but tells her little about how to go about her Saminess in the late 2000s? Perhaps for the same reasons Thomassen mobilizes biological discourses in *My Family Portrait*. Because Lundby's mother has bracketed her own Sami identity, the director intuitively turns to her own body as a way to trace what has been lost in culture.

Conclusion

Sami Blood begins with a scene in which an old Elle-Marja returns to her local community for the funeral of her younger sister Njenna. She is accompanied by her son and granddaughter and is initially both reluctant and distant, refusing to fully partake in the burial ceremony (for example, she chooses to stay alone at a hotel nearby while her son and granddaughter are lodged at her family). Through a flashback, *Sami Blood* then takes the audiences back to the 1930s, a journey that not only explains Elle-Marja's disconnect, but also allows her to eventually apologize in front of her sister's dead body and reconcile with her decision to turn her back to Saminess. Her son's and granddaughter's enthusiasm for all things Sami become instrumental in this process of reconcilement, though the younger generations are afforded very little narrative space in Kernell's film. *Sami Blood* is after all the story of the old generation who experienced blatant discrimination and racism and who either stayed (like Njenna) or left (like Elle-Marja).

In contrast, *My Family Portrait* and *Suddenly Sami* set the limelight on the children and grandchildren of the real Elle-Marjas who now try to make sense of the silences and disconnects in their families and who are eager to embrace their Sami identity. In order to reconnect with their Sami roots, Thomassen and Lundby turn to the first person film as a mode of address and use their own vulnerability in front of the camera in an attempt to re-inscribe Saminess in the national context from which it was excluded. After accidentally learning about her Sami heritage in conversation with her mother, Thomassen proclaims: 'I don't really manage to define myself as Sami, but neither as only Norwegian'. As Thomassen and Lundby work on their film projects, we see their numerous intellectual and emotional efforts to cultivate their Sami identity, a gesture prohibited by the politics of Norwegianization. They reframe personal and official archives in ways that allow them to do away with the shame experienced by Sami generations before them. In both films, photographs and videos from the national archives are intertwined with old family photographs and videos in order to underline the interplay between the director's personal story and the fate of the Sami community in a national perspective.

In addition, both directors turn to biology and genetics as important discursive resources when assuming Saminess. As I have discussed in this chapter, biology and genetics carry with them a whole range of problems that point back to the legacies of racism against the Sami. At the turn of the century, biology was mobilized to racialize the Sami, while, to date, genetics remain entangled in a complicated jargon that tells us little about how to be and become Sami in the 2010s. The question then is whether there are other ways to articulate the embodied experiences of Saminess than in biological and genetic terms? This question is for all Sami to ponder, open and closeted, members of the Sami electoral register or not, Sami by descent, Sami by affiliation, Sami by adoption, straight and LGBT Sami, urban and rural Sami, Sami men and women, young and old Sami.

Note

1 This and all the following translations from the Norwegian media are mine.

Chapter 6

Panic and migration

Envision the following scene from the Swedish film *Skörheten* (*Fragility*) (2016) by Ahang Bashi: in a high angled medium shot, we see two childhood friends, now women in their late twenties/early thirties, lying, each in her own bed, in a small apartment bedroom at night; the beds are less than a meter apart; the only source of light is from a night lamp placed on a bookshelf between the two beds; the women wear white t-shirts; their long, black hair is down; both are covered in duvets from the chest down.

AHANG BASHI: Listen, one thing, one thing I've thought about quite a lot: you and I came to Sweden when we were exactly the same age. I feel it has been much more traumatic for me than it seems to have been for you.

ROXY FARHAT: Well, I don't really have a place I feel it's home, sort of. I don't feel very connected to a particular place. It is more the people in those places. I think that it can have something to do with it. Then I also have a lot of separation anxiety. But I think that can also have something to do with having an Iranian mom [*both start laughing*] who never leaves you alone for a single second.

AHANG BASHI: Right, think if this with the separation anxiety is an Iranian thing, sort of.

ROXY FARHAT: But don't you think it is a human thing also?

AHANG BASHI: I don't know anyone else who has so much of it like we have.

ROXY FARHAT: Oh yeah ...[1]

Ahang Bashi and Roxy Farhat belong to a generation of Iranians that arrived to Sweden as very small children. Both are born in 1984 in Iran and both their families fled their war-torn home country and came to Sweden as refugees in the late 1980s. The two women speak Swedish to each other and the subject of conversation is the emotional impact of migration and separation anxiety as an 'Iranian thing'. Both Ahang and Roxy attest to experiencing anxiety, to which they then provide a sociocultural explanation. They tie it back to the migration history of their families and to cultural factors such as a specific type of Iranian motherhood. Despite the seriousness of the topic, the women manage to keep a light tone to the conversation, laughing and, later, making fun of the piece of advice Ahang received from her sister to get a family and thus cure all that separation anxiety. For as Roxy points out, 'this [to get a family] only works until the children move out', and then anxiety strikes back many times worse and much more dangerously. Impersonating an older version of herself as a mother in conversation with her children, Roxy says ironically: 'Unfortunately, I have to kill you [children] before you move out'. To this, Ahang replies: 'You do the worst Fritzl on them', referencing the morbid case of Joseph Fritzl, who held his own daughter captive for 24 years, beating and raping her, and making her give birth to seven children from his incestuous relations. As Ahang says that, both women start to laugh, yet this laughter does not absolve the gravity of their conversation. Roxy concludes pensively: 'Yeah, what else can you do?'.

This scene exemplifies how *Fragility* explores the topic of psychosocial stress experienced by children of immigrants who grew up safely in Sweden and who barely remember the escape of their parents and the arrival into the new country. The atmosphere in the scene is intimate, the tone of the conversation, honest and explorative, serious and heartfelt, but also peppered with plenty of black humour. And if Roxy admits a feeling of rootlessness and anxiety, Ahang is at times completely debilitated by panic attacks and serious depression (Figure 14). In her family, she is the only one to experience these troubling emotional states, which to Ahang is a paradox. Halfway through the film, she asks in voice-over: 'How can someone that has received so much love and protection be later torn by such unheard fear and anxiety?'. Prompted by this dilemma, she turns the camera towards herself and her family and uses filming as part of a detective work to dig deeply into her condition and find an answer to this question.

The mode of address in *Fragility* is that of the first person cinema, with Bashi functioning as both director and main character. On the one hand, *Fragility* is grounded in the director's particular family constellation and a mental struggle that Bashi does not share with her

Figure 14: Roxy comforts her friend Ahang when the latter lies in bed completely debilitated by panic attacks and depression. *Fragility* (Bashi, 2016). Cinematographers Maria Åkesson and Ahang Bashi. 2016. Courtesy of Memento Film.

siblings, not even with her best friend Roxy. On one other hand, Bashi's problems are not obsolete. Millions of people suffer from serious depression and anxiety, and millions of people have fled their native countries. This universal aspect makes *Fragility* a strong cinematic experience to others as well, who may or may not have migrated, who may or may not struggle with anxiety and depression.

In this chapter, I will analyse the emotional journey on which Bashi embarks as she thrusts herself in front of the camera. I am particularly interested in her relationships with her helpers (medical personnel, family, best friend) and how her panic attacks become inherently tied to a traumatic past she no longer remembers. Filming allows Bashi to recuperate that past and make sense of her emotional struggles not by blocking vulnerability, but by embracing it. Her answer, controversial enough, is not to do away with anxiety or think positively, as her father repeatedly suggests, but to listen to it for what it has to teach us. This makes Bashi's project quite different from other first person films analysed in this book, in particular Solveig Melkeraaen's *Good Girl*, which remains largely committed to medicalized accounts of mental struggle and where the art of not giving a damn becomes a cruelly optimistic solution for Melkeraaen (see Chapter 1). Bashi shows that she has no other option than to tune into her body and listen to her anxiety, for these tell her about a time she has long forgotten but that has been formative of who she has become as a grown-up.

Referencing an article by the French philosopher Jacques Derrida published two years before his death, Swedish anthropologist and queer theorist Don Kulick and gender scholar Jens Rydström frame vulnerability as a relationship that obliges and constrains rather than a predicament to be overcome (Kulick and Rydström 2015: 272–73). In *Fragility*, the relational dimension of vulnerability becomes particularly clear, with Bashi showing how her own vulnerability is connected to that of her best friend, her family, the political system in her country of origin, Iran, the Swedish medical system and the Swedish society at large. These relationships will receive particular attention in my analysis. Before I move on to discuss *Fragility* in detail, let me briefly address the context of increased international migration out of which Bashi's film emerges and which provides an important backdrop to her struggle.

Children, panic and migration

According to the United Nations (UN), international migration is increasing in scope, complexity and impact (UN 2016). The influx of migrants and refugees into Europe is illustrative of this. In 2015, the number of asylum applications into the European Union (EU) went up significantly, with more than a million migrants and refugees arriving in Europe by sea or over land (BBC 2016). As migration rates are getting higher, so are the numbers of migrant children crossing into Europe. A UNICEF-report shows that in 2016, children made up 16 per cent of all the migrants and refugees who arrived in Europe via the Central Mediterranean Route (from Lybia across the sea into Italy), with the vast majority of these children being unaccompanied (UNICEF Child Alert 2017). The journey from

Lybia into Italy is an extremely perilous and deadly smuggling route, claiming more than 700 children's lives in 2016 (UNICEF Child Alert 2017). In the media, no other story of migrant child death has capitalized more affect than the image of the Kurdish 3-year-old boy whose dead body was washed up on the Turkish shore on September 2015 (Lindøe 2017). This image came to epitomize the many children on the run who never make it safe to Europe and it unleashed a storm of reactions across the world. Several European leaders expressed publicly their horror, shock and compassion, yet their response did not translate into significant political action. In fact, European politicians continue to disagree as to who is to take responsibility for the new comers, children included, and how to best resettle them. It has become clear that the rise in the influx of migrants and refugees into Europe has led to a migrant crisis that tests Europeans' hospitality and feeds into already existent political, economic, national and/or cultural tensions.

When compared to other European and North American countries, Sweden has had a welcoming migration policy, taking in large numbers of migrants and refugees. As a result, immigration to Sweden reached an all-time high in 2015, with Sweden having the second highest proportion of asylum applications to its population in Europe: 1,677 for every 100,000 Swedish residents, which was almost three times more than Germany, twelve times more than Italy and 28 times more when compared to the United Kingdom (BBC 2016). Almost 163,000 people sought asylum in Sweden in 2015, of which 35,369 were unaccompanied minors (Migrationsverket 2016). The 2015 immigration peak put a strain on the Swedish Migration Agency and municipalities, and the high numbers of unaccompanied children and youth became a great challenge to the Swedish authorities (Migrationsverket 2016). In response, the Swedish Parliament voted in 2016 a more restrictive asylum policy in order to slow down the immigration pace, allow a proper handling of the applications on the roll and focus on the integration of those who have the right to reside in Sweden. At the same time, in the international press, Sweden's generous migration policy has been the target of much critique, ranging from fake news like Donald Trump's reference to a non-existent immigration-related security incident to more or less pertinent descriptions of the challenges posed by the large-scale immigration into Sweden (Nelson 2017).

Panic and anxiety are recurrent affects of the migrant crisis (Papademetriou and Banulescu-Bogdan 2016). They strike among migrants, who expose themselves to incredible perils often to be disillusioned by the way in which they are received upon their arrival in Europe. In the Norwegian documentary *Ranias flukt* (*Rania's Escape*) (Hammer, 2017), we see these affects at play as we follow the young Syrian woman, Rania Musfata Ali (aged 20) on her journey from Kobane in Syria to Austria, via Turkey, Hellas and Macedonia. *Rania's Escape* consists of a mix of Ali's own video diaries of the perilous journey and footage taken by the Norwegian director Anders Sømme Hammer in Syria, Hellas and Austria. In the beginning of August 2017, the British newspaper *The Guardian* published on its Facebook page a shorter version of Hammer's documentary entitled *Escape from Syria: Rania's Odyssey*, a video that went viral on social media, with more than 7.7 million views on *The Guardian*'s Facebook page and 79,000 shares in a month. Particularly evocative of the panic, anxiety and disillusionment experienced by Rania is the crossing of the Macedonian border, where the Macedonian police beats and teargases Rania and other migrants.

But panic and anxiety also strike among Europeans, who feel overwhelmed and even threatened by the numbers of the new comers. For example, in an interview with the Italian public broadcasting RAI on 9 July 2017, the Italian politician and President of the European Parliament Antonio Tajani made a call to other EU-countries to help Italy in dealing with the influx of migrants crossing the Mediterranean and concluded: 'If we do not confront the problem now, we will experience an influx of *biblical dimensions*' (Ording and Bruland 2017, emphasis added).[2] Tajani's biblical reference undoubtedly contributes to amplifying the statistical panic among Europeans, who, according to Tajani, in four or five years will experience an exodus of millions of migrants.

Against this backdrop, it is interesting to see how panic and migration become inherently tied in *Fragility* in ways that challenge established notions of what it means to be a child on the run. As a grown-up, Bashi suffers from panic anxiety, an emotional upheaval that she misread for a flu the first time she experienced it in her late teens. Panic in this case is an allegedly irrational response that Bashi has felt on her body for several years before she can finally tie it back to her family's escape from Iran. The focus in *Fragility* is not on the migrant children who never make it to Europe. Neither is it on the unaccompanied minors who, despite the fact that they reach their destination, risk being deported back to their home countries once they become of age. Nor it is on the 'terrorist sleepers' who harbour harmful intensions or on those disillusioned youth who become foreign fighters in Syria or Iraq.

There are other films that do that powerfully and provokingly. For example, the Norwegian documentary *De andre* (*The Others*) (2012) by the critically acclaimed filmmaker Margreth Olin showcases the tragic fates of four male unaccompanied minors whose application for residency in Norway is rejected, and who face deportation on the day they turn eighteen. The excruciating pain and disappointment these boys go through, and which Olin depicts as the moment these children are deprived of basic human rights, is hardly imaginable to Norwegian audiences, yet Olin insists on the importance of depicting that pain in a call to solidarity. Conversely, the BBC documentary *Generation Jihad* (2010) sets the spotlight on young Muslims who are born and raised in moderate Muslim families in the United Kingdom, but who turn into extremists once they are radicalized on the Internet. Here, the goal is to understand how the radicalization of these British-born young Muslims happened and to show the distress of those families that have 'nurtured' an extremist.

In comparison to documentaries like *Rania's Escape*, *The Others* or *Generation Jihad*, *Fragility* is a first person film that stays clear of extreme cases and instead fronts the story of second-generation Swedish Iranians who are neither outsiders, nor unaccompanied; neither disconnected from their ethnicity, nor radicalized. As representatives of this generation, Bashi and her friend are both Swedish and Iranian, shaped by the cultural and migration background of their parents as well as by the national and cultural norms and institutions of the country in which they grew up. That is why Bashi is willing to explore her panic attacks in a dual perspective reflective of her upbringing: both from a larger perspective of the societal pressure put on young people to succeed and from the perspective of the migration history of her family. In her panic attacks, her migrant and Swedish background make an alloy that denies easy categorizations like Swedish ethnic majority versus Iranian minority. Moreover, the film makes the migrant body relatable irrespective of the ethnic background of the viewer. It invites us to inhabit Ahang's pain as something she has in common with other ethnic Swedes who struggle. This is in itself an important ethical resource in a media landscape overflown by intensely tragic and sensational stories that commonly shock the world into helplessness and panic rather than move it into action.

If *Fragility* is not riding on sensationalism and extreme cases, it does not mean that the film lacks in emotional appeal or artistic value. The film's production, reception and circulation history demonstrate that. In 2015, the Swedish Film Institute (SFI) recognized Bashi's artistic ambitions by funding *Fragility* with 900,000 SEK through the consultant scheme (Fröberg 2017). If the domestic box office was modest, 2,303 admissions in Swedish cinemas across the country (Fröberg 2017), *Fragility* reached significantly larger audiences through broadcasting and streaming. The film was broadcast on Swedish television on three different occasions during the month of February 2017, gathering 117,000 viewings (Fröberg 2017). *Fragility* was also made available through the streaming service of the Swedish public broadcaster SVT. In addition, the film participated in several national and international film festivals, like the Bergen International Film Festival in Norway and the Göteborg Film Festival in Sweden.

Overall, the public and critical reception of the film was very positive. In 2016, *Fragility* ranked second on the list of Swedish film releases with highest review index (SFI 2017a: 8). The same year, it won Sweden's most prestigious film award, the Guldbagge, in the category Best Newcomer. In 2017, Bashi's film was awarded the top prize at the Göteborg Film Festival, where the filmmaker also received the Mai Zetterling Grant of the Artists' Board awarded to 'a film director of high artistic quality that expands the limits of short and documentary film' (Konstnärsnämnden 2017). Finally, *Fragility* was nominated for a Guldbagge in the category Best Film in 2017, which is a very important acknowledgement for a young filmmaker like Bashi. With these merits in mind, let us look closer at the film. I will begin with a discussion of Ahang's interactions with the Swedish medical personnel as she tries to make sense of her panic attacks.

Panic and the Swedish medical system

Bashi started working on the film in 2013, when her mental health deteriorated seriously (Färlin 2017). At the time, she happened to share her apartment with cinematographer Maria Åkesson, who, at Bashi's incentive, started to film her friend's mental struggle. 'I had fallen into a deep depression and did not feel I could do anything. The only thing I could do was to allow to be filmed', says Bashi at a public talk in Sweden (Wiell 2017). It is hard to watch how Ahang lies helplessly in bed as her mother and her friend Roxy try to cheer her up, yet even harder to follow her along on her interactions with the Swedish medical system. One of the emotional peaks of *Fragility* comes only a few minutes in the film. Ahang's mother, Oranus Dabestani, comes to Stockholm to help her daughter when Ahang can no longer manage on her own. When Ahang experiences a heavy anxiety attack, mother and daughter end up at the acute psychiatric ward. Camerawoman Åkesson focuses a long shot of Ahang walking slowly down the hospital corridor, but she does not follow Ahang into the doctor's office. Instead, the camera cuts to a medium shot of Ahang's worried mother in the waiting room. As the screen turns to black, we can hear a voice recording of the conversation between Ahang and the doctor. Ahang's voice sounds desperate and exhausted. She is crying throughout the entire conversation. She tells the doctor she no longer wants to live, yet protests when the latter suggests hospitalization.

AHANG: No way. It doesn't help to be placed in a hospital.
DOCTOR: Well, it may not help, but you want to take your own life.
AHANG: I don't want to take my own life.
DOCTOR: You've just said that you don't want to live.
AHANG: I don't want to live. I don't want to die either.
DOCTOR: Yes …
AHANG: I don't want to be hospitalized. I am not a sick case. It's just that I feel very bad.

When the doctor expresses his concern at Ahang's capacity to evaluate her own situation, Ahang attempts to demonstrate her determination to live by reassuring the doctor that she has been through the same situation many times. She tells him that she knows she can deal with it.

DOCTOR: Tell me, is it really so?
AHANG: Yeah, if I get a little time.
DOCTOR: Yes, you get and have time. I want to hear these words from your mouth: 'I will manage. It's hard work, but I will manage'. I want to hear this.
AHANG: I will manage. I want to survive. I have done this a thousand times.
DOCTOR: Thanks, thanks a lot! Here you go!
AHANG: But still …
DOCTOR: You have to deal with this at some point. You have to do it, once and for all. There is no shortcut.

This highly emotional conversation is edited onto a series of close-ups and medium close-ups of Ahang taking a shower and which are rendered in slow motion. Ahang's dark silhouette is projected onto a palely illuminated white-tile background, a darkness that is suggestive of her emotional turmoil and gloominess. The despair in her voice and the intensity of the situation are counteracted by the slow-motion effect and the extradiegetic sounds, which appear irregularly during the scene: slow drops of water and a slow-hand piano chord. Ahang is exposed in at least two ways: naked in the shower and emotionally wrecked in front of the doctor. The imagery is poetic, the soundtrack, simultaneously rough and carefully mixed, showing the dark and suppressive world of anxiety that makes Ahang linger between life and death: 'I don't want to live. I don't want to die'. Speaking with a foreign accent, the doctor at the acute psychiatric unit becomes the representative of a state-run medical system whose main measures for intervention remain hospitalization and medication. Although Ahang refuses to see herself as 'a sick person' ('It's just that I feel very bad'), later in the film, she introduces her 'little dose of safety', her 'emergency kit', which consists of several types of antidepressants and tranquilizers. Ahang films the pills herself in a close-up and explains how they work, concluding reconciled: 'That's life. At least for some of us'.

Pharmaceutical statistics, on the other hand, suggest that what Ahang refers as 'some of us' is in fact not a negligible number in the 2010s in Sweden. According to reports released by the Organization for Economic Co-operation and Development (OECD), Sweden's consumption rate of antidepressants increased considerably in the past decade: from 45 daily doses prescribed for every 1,000 people per day in 2000 to 92.5 daily doses in 2015 (or nearest year) (OECD 2017a: 191). This puts Sweden on the fifth position in the top-ten of OECD-countries with highest consumption of antidepressants, in the company of other Nordic countries like Iceland (ranked one) and Denmark (ranked eight) (OECD 2017a: 191). Further, statistics on pharmaceuticals collated by the Swedish National Board of Health and Welfare show that women purchase almost double as much antidepressants than men in Sweden (Socialstyrelsen 2016). Consequently, many Swedes would recognize themselves in Ahang's description of carrying along an emergency kit for depression and anxiety, either because they take antidepressants themselves or because they know someone close who takes them.

Although Ahang is open about her dependence on antidepressants, she is less willing to embrace the medical discourse that labels her a sick person, as also shown by the conversation with the doctor at the acute psychiatric ward. While pharmaceutical treatment allows Ahang to chemically control her anxiety attacks and depression, it is during individual psychotherapy that she finds an entry point into understanding her mental struggle. In the scenes filmed during therapy, the camera is commonly placed close-by to secure medium close-ups and close-ups of Ahang sitting in front of book shelves packed with psychology titles by famous psychoanalysts and psychologists like Jacques Lacan or May Rollo. Prompted to go back to her childhood years, in the first therapy scene used in the film, Ahang reflects on how her family has avoided a discussion of the psychological impact of migration on them. Instead her parents focused on the concrete details related to the escape from Iran and their arrival in Sweden. The psychologist alludes that this has affected Ahang more than her sisters, who were ten years older than Ahang at the time the family arrived in Sweden. The psychologist explains:

> A small child cannot think and process her own experiences. She can only sense. And often it is very bodily sensations that follow along. So it is possible to understand

> [anxiety], but it makes one feel crazy when one as an adult reacts almost like a baby. But in this particular case [Ahang's], it is not strange. It's important you understand this. Undoubtedly, it is a trauma to come here as a refugee and not know where you are.

It is the psychologist who suggests that Ahang's migration experiences have traumatized her as a child and that she needs help to process the trauma of migration as a grown-up. The two-and-a-half-year-old Ahang, who fled Iran with her family, has stored that trauma in her body, a bodily experience that comes to the surface many years later as anxiety and panic.

In the second therapy scene included in the film, Ahang also talks about how she finds it difficult to embrace and flag out the label of 'traumatized refugee child' without people making fun of her. Compared to the morbid and highly dramatic stories one can read of in the media, Ahang's case may appear insignificant and even illegitimate. The psychologist nevertheless encourages her to get to know better the little girl, who is an inherent part of her, which Bashi does by making *Fragility*. Thus, an important part of this first person film is to confront her family about the past they have worked so hard to put behind. From this respect, *Fragility* resonates with the Norwegian first person films by the Sami directors discussed in the previous chapter, and where filming also becomes an important tool to recuperate a denied identity. Unlike the Sami women directors, who end up turning to genetics and biology discourses to claim their Saminess, Bhasi is interested in exploring the psychosocial and cultural dimension of what makes a family not talk about an inherent part of who they are. Her interviews with her parents and two of her older sisters, as well as her interactions with her friend Roxy, are quite evocative in this sense.

Migration in two generations

Right from the start, it is clear that a supportive and loving family surrounds Ahang. The film opens with Ahang's birthday celebration where both her mother and her father give warm speeches about their strong feelings for their youngest daughter. 'I had Ahang when I was 40 and we had three big, almost grown-up children [...]. When she arrived in our lives [at war time in Shiraz, Iran], it was as if everything got young, like a sun, a sunshine', says the mother in broken Swedish. The father, Mahmood Bashi, continues: 'We are very proud of her, she is independent, very accomplished [*Ahang and her guests start laughing*]. Yes, it is just as mom said, she is a flower in our family'.

The unconditional support and love aside, it is also clear that her parents have a hard time in understanding their daughter's mental struggle. Ahang's father is an avid advocate of positive thinking and self-help. He is sceptical of psychiatrists. 'Forget about them. It's better to be your own psychiatrist', he tells his daughter. He also insistently begs Ahang to put things into perspective and think about all the achievements and good fortunes in her life. In one of the scenes, Ahang lies in bed and hears her father's words, suggestive of the impact the father has on the daughter: 'There are many people that dream to have a life like yours. And the merit is all yours. A good life and a fridge filled with food'. These repeated encouragements to be grateful and proud make it however difficult for Ahang to be able to recognize her own pain, acerbating her struggle. 'It feels bad to say that it has perhaps been a little tough for me as well', she tells both her parents.

Her mother is also a believer in the 'fortunate child' thesis advocated by Ahang's father: 'Compare yourself with the billions of people in this world and you'll see what you have', she seconds her husband. On the other hand, the mother has important reflections on how her generation had a very different way of dealing with the trauma of migration than what may be expected in Sweden in the 2010s. After carefully taking her place in front of the camera, from the family's white skin sofa, Ahang's mother, confesses in Persian:

> We come from a culture where all difficulties were to be kept away from children. We didn't want to make a big thing out of it. That is, to have to flee from home and be forced to … [*she interrupts herself without being able to continue the sentence*]. I mean, with the exception of death, God forbid, nothing more invasive can happen to a family. But in front of you, our children, we behaved as if the refugee camp was a resort. We behaved as if we were tourists. We lived in the refugee asylum for a year and a half, but it was not a good environment. Everyone who lived there had experienced horrible things. We pretended that the apartment was our home. We behaved as if we were not people who had lost everything and who had to start all over again. We kept this hidden from you.

Here, culture becomes an important variable to explain the unwillingness to talk about the emotional impact of the escape on the family. If separation anxiety was an 'Iranian thing' for Ahang and Roxy, psychologizing the family's escape must be a 'Swedish thing'. In that respect, it is worthwhile noticing that the family uses Persian at home with Swedish words interspersed in between: *deprimerad* (depressed), *ångest* (anxiety), *psykakuten* (the acute psychiatric unit), *kärlek* (love), *trygghet* (safety), *känslig* (sensitive), *terapi* (therapy) and *psykologisk* (psychological). The prevalence of Swedish vocabulary related to mental illness (and health) is striking. Of course, this reflects the realities that confront the family in Sweden as Ahang becomes ridden with anxiety and depression and needs medical help from the Swedish health system. But it also supports the cultural explanation provided by the mother, whereby Swedish is somehow better suited to psychologize than Persian.

In addition to interviewing her parents, Ahang talks to two of her older sisters. Also in these interviews, Ahang invites her sisters to take their place in the family's white skin sofa, which is symbolic of the therapeutic dimension of the conversations. First in line is Golbarg Bashi, who was thirteen at the time the family arrived in Sweden. Going back in time is also a painful affair for Golbarg. She remembers how upon their arrival into Sweden, her mother channelled all her energy into Ahang. Now a mother herself, Golbarg understands their mother's concern at the time. Nevertheless, she still finds it difficult to cope with the feeling of being put aside. 'I was supposed to be the one who kept a low profile and be silent', she tells Ahang visibly affected. On the verge of bursting into tears, Golbarg manages to control her bodily reaction by waving away the emotional intensity of the situation with a paper fan. 'I feel that thing ...' she says, and then utters the English word, 'vulnerability' in an American accent that betrays her academic and professional background (Golbarg Bashi holds a Ph.D. in Middle East Studies from Columbia University and works as a professor of Iranian studies at Rutgers University). Ahang also talks to her eldest sister, Afrodite Bashi (aka Afi), who did not follow along with the rest of family as she was about to get married in Iran. When thinking back to how the war changed their lives, Afi's heart gets heavy: '[A] s if a fear spreads throughout the body', she tells Ahang. Afi also attests to the very close ties between her and Ahang and how their separation affected her youngest sister: 'You stopped eating and you were very sad. But you got happy when I called. Mamma told me that when I called, you were happy, and afterwards you ate'.

Through conversations with her family, Ahang gets to know the 3-year-old girl who stopped eating and talking when the family arrived in Sweden, and who was too young to understand what was happening to her at the time. This journey in time allows her to accept past experiences and present struggles. As the film shows, anxiety does not miraculously disappear once Ahang recoups her past. Yet her new insights allow her to be more accepting of herself. 'Never again belittle what I have been through' and 'NO DAMN SELF HATE!' are two anxiety strategies that Ahang scribbles in her notebook towards the end of the film. The last scene of the film is of Ahang and her father watching the sunset from the balcony (Figure 15). The father still tries to sell Ahang the benefits of positive thinking by making

Figure 15: Ahang and her father watching the sunset from the balcony. *Fragility* (Bashi, 2016). Cinematographers Maria Åkesson and Ahang Bashi. 2016. Courtesy of Memento Film.

her focus on the clear skies instead of the grey clouds gathering in the horizon. The daughter gives him a warm hug, accepting his fatherly love, but not his life philosophy, which is not an option for her. Instead of chasing away her psychic fragility with positive thinking, Ahang's strategy is to accept it. Grey skies are part of life and panic attacks shall come back. Anything else but acceptance of that would be a shortcut for Ahang.

Shades of vulnerability

Fragility is an insightful commentary on the various shades of migrant vulnerability that are commonly lost in the sensationalist media discourse where migrant death has become the default attention caller. Indeed, death is the ultimate violence inflicted on a migrant body, as also Bashi's mother points out in her explanation to the daughter about how she and her husband tried to cover up the trauma of migration ('[...] death, God forbid, nothing more invasive can happen to a family'). Yet, being migrant includes many other experiences, spanning from panic, anxiety, fear, sorrow, loss and alienation to hope, relief, gratitude, joy, pride and love, only to give a few examples. These experiences also deserve our attention. And if death reduces the migrant body to an empty carcass, *Fragility* shows the shades of vulnerability that make the migrant bodies pulsate with life. The people we get to meet in the film have their own more or less effective strategies of dealing with vulnerability: black humour (Ahang and Roxy on separation anxiety), positive thinking, playing tourists or the fortunate child thesis (Ahang's parents on fleeing Iran and arriving in Sweden as refugees), waving away tears (Ahang's middle sister on being put aside), resilience (Ahang's older sister on being left behind), acceptance and making a film (Ahang on panic attacks and depression).

If the sensationalistic media discourse encourages a ranking of migrant pain and affect by flagging out extreme cases, *Fragility* legitimizes the many shades of vulnerability in between. In the film, there is no competition for who has it worst. Instead, a symphony of voices is orchestrated to convey the migration experiences of two generations: the parents who sought political asylum in Sweden as adults, and their children, whose recollection of the escape varies according to the age upon their arrival in the new country. The concertmaster in this symphonic ensemble is the second generation, as represented by Ahang and her friend Roxy. Perhaps no other scene is more symbolic of the vulnerability of this generation than when Roxy and Ahang hang out in a skatepark. Through an establishing shot, we see the two women jumping inside a half-pipe, which is a structure in a skatepark that resembles the section of a bowl-shaped swimming pool and which skaters use to ride and make aerial tricks. It is autumn in Scandinavia and the pink-blue light indicates the time is right before dawn. From the bottom of the half-pipe, Ahang and Roxy use their feet and hands in an attempt to climb up the concave walls of the half-pipe. First, Roxy speeds up in the direction of the wall, takes a few steps up until she manages to grab the top deck of the half-pipe, yet the weight of her body and her slippery shoes make her slide back to the bottom of it. Then it is Ahang's turn. The wall seems even higher this time, and Ahang stands no chance in reaching the top. Roxy gives her a push from behind, but it does not help and they both slide back. Without the traction of a skateboard (which neither Ahang nor Roxy have), it is impossible to reach the deck at the top. Their body language suggests that the two are having fun with testing their climbing skills against what seems an unbeatable obstacle. On the other hand, their play without skating gear also connotes a feeling of out-of-placeness and stuckness undergirded by the extradiegetic piano chords and the Nordic twilight. This scene in the half-pipe is a concrete visualization of vulnerability as relational, neither extreme, nor sensational, more than a lack, not necessarily an impediment.

This take on vulnerability transpires on different levels through the film, with Bashi turning her panic attacks into a fertile ground to recuperate her personal migration history, but also to connect to her family and friends as well as to criticize clinical practice and social expectations. In an interview with the Swedish newspaper *Göteborgs-Posten*, Bashi confesses:

> I hate by the way the term 'mental illness', as it implies that anxiety is classified as a sickness, as something that is wrong with you. But in fact, it is a pathfinder, the soul's way to tell you that something doesn't work. I get a lot of shit for meaning this, because it has to be classified as an illness in order for one to get help. And I get that! But it is more complex than that.
>
> (Färlin 2017)

In this quote, like in Ahang's conversation with the doctor at the acute psychiatric ward discussed earlier in this chapter ('I am not a sick person. It's just that I feel very bad'), there lies a critique of how intense negative emotions like anxiety are commonly pathologized in the clinical discourse. This does not mean that Ahang belittles the importance of having a responsive medical system that can provide necessary help in the form of among others medication. After all, she is grateful of her 'emergency kit' that allows her to chemically control her anxiety and depression. But if pharmaceuticals provide a temporary fix, Ahang is looking for more long-term solutions that take into account the psychosocial stress of the patient. That is why she treats anxiety as a pathfinder not only into her past, but also into her future. This process takes time, and time costs money in a medical system pressured to deliver quick results, which explains why Ahang asks the doctor at the acute psychiatric unit for more time: '[…] if I get a little time […] I will manage. I want to survive. I have done this a thousand times'.

On other occasions, Bashi criticizes social norms and expectations in the contemporary Swedish society: 'It is not so strange that so many people are depressed in our society, which puts so much pressure on people to be happy. To be just a little different makes it easy for us to feel worthless – it is not easy to be healthy in a sick society' (Magnusson 2016). Through her film, Ahang confronts the unrealistic expectations of being 'so damn strong and good all the time', as she writes in her notebook when listing possible causes for her anxiety. From this light, it becomes clear why she chooses to entitle her film *Fragility*. The film is a call to accept psychic fragility or what in this book I have called vulnerability.

If acceptance of vulnerability is her long-term strategy, as a filmmaker, she has found another short-term strategy to survive when depression, panic and anxiety raid at their worse. In the media, Bashi confesses: 'I felt that if I filmed, it was not entirely meaningless. The camera became an instrument to manage throughout the days, a prime mover to get out of bed' (Dahlman 2016). And elsewhere, 'I also noticed that I felt better when the camera was with me. I could be very low, but if I decided to take the camera with me to my meeting with the psychologist, then chances were that I would go. Otherwise I would have stayed at home' (Mattsson 2016). That said, *Fragility* is not a hymn to the power of the camera to initiate change and partake in therapy, but a call to solidarity and community with those who struggle, irrespective of their migrant or medical history.

Conclusion

In *Fragility*, Bashi fronts her own experience with panic attacks and migration in an attempt to understand. Her first person film is not goal-orientated, but systemic, showing how Ahang deals with her problems on a daily basis, for three years. Sometimes, she is confident, other times, she slides back at the bottom of the half-pipe, to use one of the metaphors suggested by the film. Bashi's story is neither sensational, nor extreme, yet very effective in depicting the deep impact of migration on two generations. The source of Bashi's pain is, like for the rest of her family, the escape from a war-torn and oppressive Iran. Yet, unlike the rest of her family, her pain manifests herself in the language of anxiety and panic, a language that she shares with many other Swedes. Bashi's specific migration story left aside, her struggle is thus also recognizable to others who do not have a migrant background, but who, like Ahang, consciously or unconsciously rumble under the burden of the psychosocial stress in contemporary Sweden. In this way, *Fragility* makes it possible for viewers to inhabit Ahang's pain, yet with a clear understanding of the migrant perspective that Bashi brings to the fore. The fact that she embraces her migrant history does not make her less Swedish. She is one of us while she is both Iranian and Swedish, neither an outsider, nor a sleeper, but a young, talented director with a history behind and many other stories to tell.

The aesthetics of vulnerability in *Fragility* are not of the collage, as could be seen in *Good Girl* (see Chapter 1) or of the close-up, as in *Ida's Diary* (see Chapter 4), but of nuances provided through the camera's dwelling on anxiety as a psychosocial phenomenon. Occasionally, like in the highly emotional scene at the acute psychiatric ward, the camera is turned off, while the sound continues to document Ahang's panic and anxiety as she lingers between life and death. Whether visible in front of the camera or audible on the soundtrack of the film in the real-time audiorecordings from the psychiatric ward and in voice-over commentaries, Bashi exposes herself not in isolation from others, but in interaction with them, be that medical personnel, family or best friends. It is in these encounters that the ethical content of *Fragility* is provided. Whether we are in Ahang's bedroom, at the acute psychiatric ward, in the family's white skin sofa or in a half-pipe, we are made to see the interhuman dimension of vulnerability and how (mental) struggle can bring people together rather than tear them apart. In this way, *Fragility* couldn't be a more appropriate theoretical object to end this book about first person films staging vulnerability in contemporary Scandinavia.

Notes

1 This and all the following translations from the film are mine.
2 This and all the following translations from the Norwegian and Swedish media are mine.

Conclusion

Exposing vulnerability: A call to responsiveness

In the first person films by Scandinavian women filmmakers discussed in this book, the exposure of vulnerability is a call to responsiveness on the part of the viewer. As viewers, we are not simply fed spectacles of vulnerability, but also made aware of our role in other people's pain once we sit down in front of the screen. The vulnerabilities of the women filmmakers elicit a vulnerability in the viewers that oftentimes blocks empathy and instead stimulates a critical disposition through other less 'noble' affective responses like frustration, confusion, contempt, irritation, deception, disappointment and even disgust. In this way, the pain of others does not become ours, although we clearly experience our commonality and interconnectedness with those who are exposed on the screen.

In a contribution to the edited volume *Vulnerability in Resistance*, Marianne Hirsch shows how the forms of responsiveness and vulnerability fostered by aesthetic encounters attune us 'to the needs of the present, to the potentialities of change, and to the future' (2016: 82). Likewise, the films analysed in this book are not past-oriented, not even a film like *Brothers* in which the director seeks to encapsulate childhood in real time. Instead, they are acutely present in our contemporaneity, covering highly relevant topics such as mental health, bullying, childhood and parenthood in a digital age, racism and migration. They are future-oriented not because they provide a convincing recipe for change. Most of them in fact do not, but because they move us, literally and emotionally, towards what Hirsch described as 'an ethics and a politics of open-endedness and mobility' (2016: 82). The optics that allows this move is the first person film as a mode of address.

Inspired by the work of Alicia Lebow (2012) and her colleagues, this book has attended to the various forms of first person filmmaking in a specific time (2009–16) and geographic area (Norway and Sweden), and by a specific group of filmmakers (women). All the films analysed in this book utilize a collage of representation forms that mix life and art, the fictional and the real, the staged and the spontaneous. In *Good Girl*, Solveig Melkeraaen moves between aesthetic extremes, from raw, intimate and unpolished footage of herself, like for example the scene in which she receives electroshock, to stylized, self-ironic footage in which she depicts herself as an absurdly successful woman filmmaker or an overweight ballerina who fails to perform a perfect spin.

Brothers is a selection made out of hundreds of hours of real-time footage that Aslaug Holm shot of her two sons for eight years. It is the most time-consuming first person film discussed in this book, taking the parent director Holm almost a decade to complete. What to other parents remains a personal archive of special occasions, to Holm was a life film project that shows the high stakes of being the director in charge as well as the mother of the two boys.

In *The Reunion*, Anna Odell chooses a peculiar and quite innovative form of cinematic figuration. She uses her own experiences with bullying in school to make a film in two parts. *Part One: The Speech* is fiction, a hypothesis of what could have happened, had Odell been invited to her twentieth class reunion. *Part Two: The Meetings* is a re-enactment of the conversations Odell had with her former colleagues after she showed them *Part One: The Speech*. Unlike in the other first person films discussed in this book, except Odell, who plays herself, the rest of the cast consists of two teams of professional actors, one team performing in *Part One: The Speech*, and the other in *Part Two: The Meetings*. While Odell encouraged her actors to tap into their own school memories, *The Reunion* is first and foremost an expression of Odell's own experiences with bullying and an example of her provoking and generically hard to define first person art in which the speaking 'I' confronts and challenges established societal and aesthetic norms.

Ida's Diary is another example of a first person film that does not comfortably fit the denomination 'autobiographical'. The film is the result of an intriguing collaboration between Ida Storm and the director August Baugstø Hanssen and his team. *Ida's Diary* consists of Storm's video diary entries in the period 2006 to 2013, in which she thematizes her struggle with borderline personality disorder and self-harm. In 2009, after Storm contacts the production house Indie Film, Hanssen takes directorial control over Storm's raw material and continues the collaboration with her for five years until the release of the film. This means that Storm delegates artistic control of her story to a professional film team, a strategic move that has at least two consequences. First, Hanssen and his technical team cultivate a cinematic language that allows viewers to feel Ida's pain and scars on their bodies rather than watch them from a distance. Second, the film gives Storm the opportunity to front her case as a way to call for acceptance for youth who struggle.

Suddenly Sami by Ellen-Astri Lundby and *My Family Portrait* by Yvonne Thomassen are first person films that show us the directors' entangled way to recuperate a Sami identity that their parents and grandparents have kept hidden from them as a result of racism and blatant discrimination. In both films, photographs and videos from the national archives are intertwined with old family photographs and personal videos in order to underline the interplay between the director's personal story and the fate of the Sami community in a national perspective. Through the first person film as a mode of address, Lundby and Thomassen seek to redefine the shame that many Sami came to internalize. They also find ways to reconnect with their Sami roots in a discursive landscape in which the legacy of racism continues to permeate contemporary struggles over what it means to be Sami.

Finally, in *Fragility*, Ahang Bashi mobilizes the first person film as a mode of address in order to find the cause of her anxiety and panic attacks. Almost immediately, filming herself and her family becomes a detective endeavour into her family's history of migration from a war-torn Iran to Sweden in the 1980s, and which Bashi does not remember. In addition, filming partakes in the therapy process by giving meaning to the depression ridden periods and by keeping the director motivated to continue therapy and not to give up. Most of the times, the camera is on, but there are also situations in which only the sound is recorded, like in the highly emotional scene at the acute psychiatric ward where we can hear Bashi lingering between life and death.

These different types of first person cinematic figuration generate their own ethical content, with all the films discussed in this book initiating a process of interrogation in the viewer. I will not reiterate here the ethical dimension of each film, simply because a brief summary cannot do justice to the nuances and complexities at play in my corpus. Instead, I want to make some remarks about the cultural perspectives provided by the first person films of the Scandinavian women filmmakers. What do these films tell us about how Scandinavians configure the self in the 2000s?

In the introductory chapter, I pointed out how the ideology of state individualism has historically been central to how Scandinavians have constructed their identity in the post-war period. According to Swedish historians Henrik Berggren and Lars Trägårdh (2006), state individualism is an ideology of state in which a strong, interventionist state is seen as an asset, and not a hindrance, to individualism. This way of conceiving of the strong state and individualism as mutually inclusive is typical of the Nordic countries and is in stark contrast to the neo-liberal state ideology, in which the state must necessarily be restrained for the individuals to remain autonomous. In her research on vulnerability, American legal theorist and political philosopher Martha A. Fineman (2013) criticizes this latter conception of the restrained state found among others in the United States. Instead, Fineman emphasizes the universal dimension of vulnerability and advocates for a 'responsive state' that takes an active role in lessening, ameliorating and compensating for individual vulnerability, 'providing us with the resilience or resources with which to address and confront misfortune and opportunity' (2013: 22). In this way, Fineman seeks to dissolve the antagonism between the strong state and autonomous individuals permeating the American sociopolitical and cultural context, an ideological move that is in line with the Scandinavian notion of state individualism. Given the specific sociopolitical and cultural differences between Scandinavia and the United States, how do the Scandinavian first person films by women filmmakers engage with the tenet of state individualism? My corpus affords important reflections starting from this question, although my analyses first and foremost direct attention to vulnerability as a multifaceted and ambivalent condition inscribed in the first person films by Scandinavian women filmmakers. Let me therefore end this conclusory chapter by outlining some reflections on the question of state individualism.

From different perspectives and to various degrees, the first person films by Scandinavian women filmmakers launch a critique of the lack of responsiveness on the part of the strong Nordic welfare state by showing the more problematic and darker sides of living in Scandinavia. This critique is anchored in the flesh and experiences of each of the women filmmakers discussed in this book, without their films embracing an explicitly feminist agenda. Rather, their female bodies become an arena to stage the discontents of Scandinavian individuals that continue to see the faulty strong state as part of a solution rather than a problem. After all, the films discussed in this book have received financial support from state institutions like the Norwegian Film Institute and the Swedish Film Institute, although the realities they construct are very different from the hygge brand promoted abroad through Scandinavian interior design and lifestyle.

Good Girl, *Ida's Diary* and *Fragility* invite a critical look at the mental health system in a region otherwise known for generous state-funded health care and for ranking at the top of the World Happiness Report (Helliwell et al. 2017 and 2018). In these three films, we see the women receiving immediate help at the acute psychiatric ward in the form of medication and hospitalization, yet a long-term follow-up seems to be lacking. It appears that the state is in search of a quick fix to mental struggles, while the patients themselves need more time, as Bashi begs for in conversation with the doctor at the acute psychiatric ward. For Melkeraaen, Storm and Bashi, filming becomes a way to stretch out time and deal with quite complex diagnoses in ways that the Nordic state medical system does not afford. The camera compensates for the lack of responsiveness on the part of the state, a substitution that however brings along a new set of ethical dilemmas. This becomes particularly clear in *Good Girl*, where filming is both affirming and profoundly threatening at the same time.

The state-funded educational system is also under critical consideration. In *The Reunion*, Odell makes an important point about how bullying in public schools was tacitly accepted in the good faith that children could do no big harm ('They are only children', the adults in charge used to say). This attitude among teachers and other adults acerbated Odell's suffering to the point that she considered suicide. In *Brothers*, school activities are often depicted as boring and coercive. Children's strength and independence is caged by institutional expectations that fail to see childhood as a fully-fledged existence and instead treat it as a transitional phase towards adulthood. Although *Ida's Diary* does not include any video footage from school, Storm mentions in her video diaries how failing schoolwork increases her emotional turmoil and affects negatively her already shaken sense of self-esteem. Here as well, the school is depicted as unresponsive to Storm's needs, aggravating her struggle. In an attempt to prevent others from having the same fate, Storm uses the film to launch a campaign in which she calls for the introduction of mental health as a separate subject in public schools.

Most sceptical of the strong Nordic state are the women filmmakers with a Sami background. In *Suddenly Sami* and *My Family's Portrait*, archival material is used to underline how the Norwegian state historically projected vulnerability onto the Sami minority in an attempt to contain it. The state, represented by institutions such as the school and the church, took upon itself the task to 'civilize' the Sami by using intrusive measures, which in the long run resulted in a debilitating shame that made several generations of Sami turn their back to their Sami identity. Under the pretext of responsiveness, the strong state sought to assimilate the Sami by wiping their language and their traditions.

Both Lundby and Thomassen mention how Sami children were forcefully sent to Norwegian boarding schools in which it was forbidden to speak Sami or manifest any other aspect of their Sami culture, perhaps with the exception of wearing traditional Sami clothes. In *Suddenly Sami*, for example, Lundby uses among others a clip from the German film *Eine reise unter der Mitternachtssonne* ('A journey under the midnight sun') (Prager, 1931). Most likely filmed in a school in the Sami community of Karasjok in northern Norway (Johansen 2017), the clip shows us a small Sami girl dressed in traditional clothes learning how to spell the Norwegian word *mor* (mother) under the supervision of the teacher. She is hesitant and insecure, constantly seeking the confirmation of the teacher, who stands next to her and guides her when she first spells the word wrongly. Lundby uses this archival material from the interwar period to reconstruct her mother's experiences in boarding school and to emphasize the oppressive nature of this educational system. In voice-over, she says: 'When mom was 7–8 years old, she started in a boarding school. By taking the children away from home, the Norwegian state apparatus got an effective tool in the Norwegianization of the Sami'.

Fragility also takes the perspective of an ethnic minority, this time with a more recent migration history to the Nordic region: the Iranians that came to Sweden as refugees in the 1980s. *Fragility* is less interested in reflecting on the position of the Swedish welfare state vis-à-vis its minorities. The film's focus is first and foremost on Bashi's family and how they dealt with the escape from the oppressive regime in Iran after their arrival in Sweden. Yet, the Swedish welfare state is also lurking in the background in *Fragility*, particularly in the conversations between Bashi and her parents. Her mother talks about the difficult times in the refugee camp, while her father asks her to show gratitude for what she has been able to achieve in Sweden. The father's insistence on gratitude alludes in subtle ways to national discourses in Sweden, and Scandinavia, that ask migrants to be grateful for the way in which the welfare state has minimized their vulnerability by granting them residence permit. For a bicultural child like Bashi, however, this discourse of gratitude is difficult to accept. Instead, she flags out her vulnerability as a child of migrants and as a young woman with panic anxiety, resisting conventional ideas that migrants must be grateful and that mental struggle must necessarily be a problem. In this way, Bashi's double vulnerability (a young woman with an immigrant background ridden by panic attacks) becomes a resource for resistance, if not a resource for immediate social transformation.

This sociopolitical and cultural specificity left aside, the Scandinavian first person films by and with women filmmakers speak of human experiences recognizable to more than just Scandinavians. Each chapter has highlighted the global prevalence of the topics approached in these films by among others referencing statistics. Millions of people around the world are affected by depression and panic anxiety. Hundreds of thousands of migrants have fled to Europe in search of better lives. Millions of parents and children deal on an everyday basis with the dilemmas of growing up in a digital age. Bullying remains a frequent behaviour among children and youth in schools and online, while self-harm is on the rise both among girls and boys in the West. The reflections put forward in this book are therefore also relevant to global audiences that may or may not have a particular interest in Scandinavia. *Exposing Vulnerability* highlights that Scandinavians construct meaning in their lives, not in splendid and exceptional isolation from the rest of world, but very much in conversation with it.

References

Aalen, Kristin (2016), 'Gullrute-pris til klipper Erik Andersson fra Stavanger', *Stavanger Aftenblad*, 18 May, p. 32.

Aas, Einar K. and Zapffe, Peter W. (eds) ([1942] 1995), *Vett og uvett: Stubber fra Troms og Nordland*, Trondheim: Bruns Forlag.

Aasheim, Anette (2014), 'Hun var så flink', *A-Magasinet*, 15 August, pp. 7–10.

Ahmed, Sara (2004a), *The Cultural Politics of Emotion*, Edinburgh: Edinburgh University Press.

——— (2004b), 'Affective economies', *Social Text*, 22:2, pp. 117–39.

Anderson, Laurie (1982), 'Let X=X/It Tango', *Big Science*, CD, USA: Warner Bros. Records.

Anthony, Andrew (2015), 'Karl Ove Knausgaard: "Writing is a way of getting rid of shame"', *The Guardian*, 1 March, https://www.theguardian.com/books/2015/mar/01/karl-ove-knausgaard-interview-shame-dancing-in-the-dark. Accessed 11 October 2017.

A-magasinet (2015), 'Dagboknotatene', 9 October, pp. 7–10.

Associated Press in Stockholm (2013), 'Swedish cinemas take aim at gender bias with Bechdel test rating', *The Guardian*, 6 November, http://www.theguardian.com/world/2013/nov/06/swedish-cinemas-bechdel-test-films-gender-bias. Accessed 11 October 2017.

Aufderheide, Pat, Jaszi, Peter and Chandra, Mridu (2009), 'Honest truths: Documentary filmmakers on ethical challenges in their work', *Center for Media and Social Impact*, http://www.cmsimpact.org/making-your-media-matter/documents/best-practices/honest-truths-documentary-filmmakers-ethical-chall. Accessed 11 October 2017.

Backer, Stina (2009), 'On trial for faking madness – As part of an artwork', *The Independent*, 30 August, http://www.independent.co.uk/news/world/europe/on-trial-for-faking-madness-ndash-as-part-of-an-artwork-1779651.html. Accessed 11 October 2017.

Bal, Mieke (2013), 'Lexicon for cultural analysis', in A. Babka, D. Finzi, and C. Ruthner (eds), *Die Lust an der Kultur-Theorie: Transdisziplinäre Interventionen. Für Wolfgang Müller-Funk*, Vienna and Berlin: Turia + Kant Verlag, pp. 49–81.

BBC (2016), 'Migrant crisis: Migration to Europe explained in seven charts', 4 March, http://www.bbc.com/news/world-europe-34131911. Accessed 12 October 2017.

Berggren, Henrik and Trägårdh, Lars (2006), *Är svensken människa?: Gemenskap och oberoende i det moderna Sverige*, Stockholm: Nordstedt.

Berg-Nordlie, Mikkel and Skogvang, Susann F. (2016), 'Sametingets valgmanntall', Store Norske Leksikon, https://snl.no/Sametingets_valgmanntall. Accessed 12 October 2017.

Berlant, Lauren (2011), *Cruel Optimism*, Durham, NC: Duke University Press.

Bertheussen, Linn (2014), 'Filmet sin egen depresjon', *iTromsø*, 15 October, http://www.itromso.no/kultur/article10233782.ece. Accessed 12 October 2017.

Bie, Nanok (2013), 'Tonåringar dömda för förtal på Instagram', SVT, 25 June, https://www.svt.se/nyheter/inrikes/instagram-goteborg. Accessed 12 October 2017.

Bjerkeland, Ingvild and Kielland, Johanne S. (2015), *Hovedkarakterer i norsk kinofilm i perioden 2011-2015 i et kjønnsperspektiv: En kvantitativ undersøkelse*, Oslo: Norsk Skuespillerforbund, http://www.skuespillerforbund.no/images/downloads/Hovedkarakterer_i_norsk_film.pdf. Accessed 12 October 2017.

Borland, Sophie (2016), 'More children are self-harming due to social media: Number who admit cutting themselves up by 14% in two years', *Daily Mail Online*, 9 December, http://www.dailymail.co.uk/news/article-4015620/More-children-self-harming-social-media.html. Accessed 12 October 2017.

Butler, Judith (2004), *Precarious Life: The Powers of Mourning and Violence*, London and New York: Verso.

——— (2009), *Frames of War: When Is Life Grievable?*, London and New York: Verso.

——— (2016), 'Rethinking vulnerability and resistance', in J. Butler, Z. Gambetti and L. Sabsay (eds), *Vulnerability in Resistance*, Durham, NC and London: Duke University Press, pp. 12–27.

Butler, Judith and Gambetti, Zeynep (2013), 'Rethinking vulnerability and resistance: Feminism and social change', Columbia Social Difference, http://socialdifference.columbia.edu/projects/rethinking-vulnerability-feminism-social-change. Accessed 12 October 2017.

Butler, Judith, Gambetti, Zeynep and Sabsay, Leticia (eds) (2016), *Vulnerability in Resistance*, Durham, NC and London: Duke University Press.

Campbell, Denis (2016), 'NHS-figures show "shocking" rise in self-harm among young', *The Guardian*, 23 October, https://www.theguardian.com/society/2016/oct/23/nhs-figures-show-shocking-rise-self-harm-young-people. Accessed 12 October 2017.

Choi, Jinhee and Frey, Mattias (2014), 'Introduction', in J. Choi and M. Frey (eds), *Cine-Ethics: Ethical Dimensions of Film Theory, Practice, and Spectatorship*, New York and London: Routledge, pp. 1–14.

Clift, Robert A. (2014), 'Uncomfortable viewing: Deauthorized performances, ethics, and spectatorship in Sacha Baron Cohen's *Borat*', in J. Choi and M. Frey (eds), *Cine-Ethics: Ethical Dimensions of Film Theory, Practice, and Spectatorship*, New York and London: Routledge, pp. 96–110.

Cohn, Pamela (2014), 'Three in one: Director, freak, artist', *DOX: European Documentary Magazine*, 101, http://www.doxmagazine.com/three-in-onedirector-freak-artist/. Accessed 12 October 2017.

Dahlman, Elin (2016), 'Kameran tog Ahang Bashi genom krisen', *Gotlands Tidninga*, 15 September, p. 36.

Dancus, Adriana Margareta (2013), 'Male mental illness and Norwegian compassion: A study of *Elling* (2001) and *The art of negative thinking* (2006)', *NORMA – Nordic Journal for Masculinity Studies*, 8:1, pp. 7–25.

——— (2016), 'Women, vulnerability and depression: The cruel optimism of not giving a damn in *Good Girl*', *Journal of Scandinavian Cinema*, 6:2, pp. 137–51.

——— (2017), 'Å filme sine dype arr: (Selv)mediering og selvskading i *Idas dagbok* (2014)', in C. Hamm, S. H. Lindøe and B. Markussen (eds), *Lidelsens estetikk. Sår, sorg og smerte i litteratur, film og medier*, Bergen: Alvheim & Eide Akademisk Forlag, pp. 141–58.

Daney, Serge (2004), 'The tracking shot in *Kapo*', *Senses of Cinema,* 30, http://sensesofcinema.com/2004/feature-articles/kapo_daney/. Accessed 12 October 2017.

Desta, Yohana (2018), 'The Hollywood wage gap isn't getting better - but actresses are pushing back', *Vanity Fair,* 19 January, https://www.vanityfair.com/hollywood/2018/01/hollywood-wage-gap-times-up. Accessed 28 November 2018.

Dunham, Lena (2014), *Not That Kind of Girl: A Young Woman Tells You What She's 'Learned'*, London: Fourth Estate.

Egedius, Tonje (2014), 'Hvorfor er kvinner mer borte fra jobben enn menn?', *Aftenposten*, 17 October, http://www.aftenposten.no/amagasinet/Hvorfor-er-kvinner-mer-borte-frajobben-enn-menn-7725977.html. Accessed 12 October 2017.

Eidsvåg, Terje (2014), 'Flink pike får elektrosjokk', *Adresseavisen*, 9 October, http://www.adressa.no/kultur/article10214148.ece. Accessed 12 October 2017.

'expose, v.' (2017), *Merriam-Webster Online*, Springfield, MA: Encyclopedia Britannica, https://www.merriam-webster.com/dictionary/expose. Accessed 12 October 2017.

Film & Kino (2014), *Årbok 2014*, http://www.kino.no/incoming/article1214127.ece/binary/Film%20%20Kino%20-%20%C3%85rbok%202014.pdf. Accessed 12 June 2018.

——— (2015), *Årbok 2015*, http://www.kino.no/incoming/article1267859.ece/binary/Film%20%20Kino%20-%20Årbok%202015.pdf. Accessed 12 June 2018.

Fineman, Martha A. (2013), 'Equality, autonomy, and the vulnerable subject in law and politics', in M.A. Fineman and A. Grear (eds), *Vulnerability: Reflections on a New Foundation for Law and Politics*, Farnham: Ashgate, pp. 13–28.

Fineman, Martha A. and Grear, Anna (eds) (2013), *Vulnerability: Reflections on a New Foundation for Law and Politics*, Farnham: Ashgate.

Frame, Janet ([1961] 1980), *Faces in the Water*, London: Women's Press.

Friends (2018), *Friendsrapporten 2018*, Solna: Friends, https://friends.se/wp-content/uploads/2018/08/friendsrapporten-2018.compressed.pdf. Accessed 3 December 2018.

Fröberg, Johan (2017), e-mail to author, 18 May.

Färlin, Mårten (2017), '"DET VAR I FLYKTEN MIN SKÖRHET BLEV TILL"', *Göteborgs Posten Två Dagar*, 6 May, pp. 10–12.

Geddes, Linda (2014), 'Does sharing photos of your children on Facebook put them at risk?', *The Guardian*, 21 September, https://www.theguardian.com/technology/2014/sep/21/children-privacy-online-facebook-photos. Accessed 12 October 2017.

Gerrard, Meg and Houlihan, Amy E. (2008), 'Perceived vulnerability', National Cancer Institute, Division of Cancer Control and Population Sciences, 28 April, http://cancercontrol.cancer.gov/brp/research/constructs/perceived_vulnerability.html. Accessed 12 October 2017.

Gilson, Erinn C. (2014), *The Ethics of Vulnerability: A Feminist Analysis of Social Life and Practice*, New York: Routledge.

Grønstad, Asbjørn (2016), *Film and the Ethical Imagination*, London: Palgrave MacMillan.

Haarder, Jon Helt (2014), *Performativ biografisme: En hovedstrømning i det senmodernes skandinaviske litteratur*, Copenhagen: Gyldendal.

Helliwell, John, Layard, Richard and Sachs, Jeffrey (2017), *World Happiness Report 2017*, New York: Sustainable Development Solutions Network, http://worldhappiness.report/ed/2017/. Accessed 12 October 2017.

——— (2018), *World Happiness Report 2018*, New York: Sustainable Development Solutions Network, http://worldhappiness.report/ed/2018/. Accessed 27 November 2018.

Helsedirektoratet (The Norwegian Directorate of Health) (2014), *Handlingsplan for forebygging av selvmord og selvskading 2014-2017*, https://helsedirektoratet.no/publikasjoner/handlingsplan-for-forebygging-av-selvmord-og-selvskading-20142017. Accessed 12 October 2017.

Hernes, Helga M. (1987), *Welfare State and Woman Power: Essays in State Feminism*, Oslo: Norwegian University Press.

——— (2004), 'Statsfeminisme – et personlig tilbakeblikk', *Nytt Norsk Tidsskrift*, 21:3&4, pp. 288–93.

Higonnet, Anne (1998), *The History and Crisis of Ideal Childhood*, London: Thames & Hudson.

Hilton, Claire (2007), 'An exploration of the patient's experience of electro-convulsive therapy in mid-twentieth century creative literature: A historical study with implications for practice today', *Journal of Affective Disorders*, 97:1, pp. 5–12.

Hirsch, Marianne (2016), 'Vulnerable times', in J. Butler, Z. Gambetti and L. Sabsay (eds), *Vulnerability in Resistance*, Durham, NC and London: Duke University Press, pp. 76–96.

Hirshbein, Laura (2012), 'Historical essay: Electroconvulsive therapy, memory and self in America', *Journal of the History of Neuroscience*, 21:2, pp. 147–69.

Hjort, Mette (2005), *Small Nation, Global Cinema: The New Danish Cinema*, Minneapolis, MN: University of Minnesota Press.

——— (2010), *Lone Scherfig's Italian for Beginners*, Seattle: University of Washington Press.

Holst, Cathrine (ed.) (2002), *Kjønnsrettferdighet: Utfordringer for feministisk politikk*, Oslo: Gyldendal akademisk.

Hostad, Odd (2014), 'Lett om tungt tema', *Romsdals budstikke*, 10 October, http://www.rbnett.no/kultur/film/article10217449.ece. Accessed 19 October 2017.

Huitfeldt, Anniken (2012), 'Et hysj-hysj tema?', NRK, 4 October, http://www.nrk.no/ytring/hvorfor-kvinner-er-mer-sykemeldt-1.8346598. Accessed 19 October 2017.

Hustvedt, Siri (2016), 'No competition', in S. Hustvedt, *A Woman Looking at Men Looking at Women: Essays on Art, Sex, and the Mind*, New York: Simon & Schuster, pp. 79–95.

Hutchinson, Pamela (2018), '#MeToo and Hollywood: What's changed in the industry a year on?', *The Guardian*, 8 October, https://www.theguardian.com/world/2018/oct/08/metoo-one-year-on-hollywood-reaction. Accessed 28 November 2018.

'hygge, n.' (2017), *OED Online*, Oxford: Oxford University Press, https://en.oxforddictionaries.com/definition/hygge. Accessed 19 October 2017.

Ingebritsen, Christine (2002), 'Norm entrepreneurs: Scandinavia's role in world politics', *Cooperation and Conflict*, 37:1, pp. 11–23.

Isachsen, Sophie E. (2016), *Forbilde*, Oslo: Cappelen Damm.

James, Carrie (2014), *Disconnected: Youth, New Media, and the Ethics Gap*, Cambridge, MA: The MIT Press.

Jarvi, Stephanie S., Jackson, Benita, Swenson, Lance and Crawford, Heather (2013), 'The impact of social contagion on non-suicidal self-injury: A review of literature', *Archives of Suicide Research*, 17:1, pp. 1–19.

Jensen, Knut E. (2015), in conversation with Aslaug Holm, The National Library of Norway, Oslo, 30 November.

Jerslev, Anne (2004), *Vi ses på TV: Medier og intimitet*, København: Gyldendal.

Jerslev, Anne and Gade, Rune (eds) (2005), *Performative Realism: Interdisciplinary Studies in Art and Media*, Copenhagen: Museum Tusculanum Press.

Jimerson, Shane R., Swearer, Susan M. and Espelage, Dorothy L. (eds) (2010), *Handbook of Bullying Schools: An International Perspective*, New York: Routledge.

Johansen, Elin (2017), e-mail to author, 27 October.

Kang, Inkoo (2016), 'How the Swedish Film Institute achieved 50-50 funding distribution between male and female directors', *IndieWire*, 18 February, http://www.indiewire.com/2016/02/how-the-swedish-film-institute-achieved-50-50-funding-distribution-between-male-and-female-directors-204741/. Accessed 19 October 2017.

Katz, John S. and Katz, Judith M. (1991), 'Ethics and the perception of ethics in autobiographical film', in L. Gross, J. Katz and J. Ruby (eds), *Image Ethics: The Moral Rights of Subjects in Photographs, Film and Television*, New York: Oxford University Press, pp. 119–34.

Kesey, Ken ([1962] 1973), *One Flew over the Cuckoo's Nest*, London: Picador.

Knausgård, Karl O. (2009–11), *Min kamp*, Oslo: Oktober.

Knudsen, Britta T. and Thompsen, Bodil M. S. (2002), *Virkelighedshunger: Nyrealismen i visuel optic: antologi*, Copenhagen: Tiderne Skifter.

Koivunen, Anu, Kyrölä, Katariina and Ryberg, Ingrid (eds) (2018), *The Power of Vulnerability: Mobilizing Affect in Feminist Queer and Anti-Racist Media Cultures*, Manchester: Manchester University Press.

Konstnärsnämnden (2017), 'Mai Zetterling-stipendiet', https://www.konstnarsnamnden.se/default.aspx?id=11726. Accessed 19 October 2017.

Kulick, Don and Rydström, Jens (2015), *Loneliness and Its Opposite: Sex, Disability, and the Ethics of Engagement*, Durham, NC and London: Duke University Press.

Kulås, Guri (2015), 'Verd å få med seg frå 2015', *Klassekampen*, 10 December, pp. 30–31.

Kvist, Roger (1994), 'The racist legacy in modern Swedish Saami policy', *Canadian Journal of Native Studies*, 14:02, pp. 203–20.

Kyllingstad, Jon R. (2012), 'Norwegian physical anthropology and the idea of a Nordic master race', *Current Anthropology*, 53:05, pp. 46–56.

——— (2014), *Measuring the Master Race: Physical Anthropology in Norway 1890–1945*, Cambridge: OpenBook Publishers.

Lane, Jim (2002), *The Autobiographical Documentary in America*, Madison, WI: University of Wisconsin Press.

Lange, Ariane (2016), 'How this woman changed gender inequality in Swedish films', *BuzzFeed*, 27 April, https://www.buzzfeed.com/arianelange/sweden-film-gender?utm_term=.ahndNp7jE#.fhzKnVDbo. Accessed 24 October 2017.

Larsson, Lisbeth (2010), 'Självbiografi, autofiktion, testimony, lifewriting', *Tidskrift för genusvetenskap*, 4, pp. 7–21.

——— (2016), 'The return and transformations of true stories', *The History of Nordic Women's Literature*, 13 October, https://nordicwomensliterature.net/2016/10/13/the-return-and-transformations-of-true-stories/. Accessed 24 October 2017.

Lauzen, Martha M. (2018), *The Celluloid Ceiling: Behind-the-Scenes Employment of Women on the Top 100, 250, and 500 Films of 2017*, San Diego: Center for the Study of Women in Television and Film, San Diego State University, https://womenintvfilm.sdsu.edu/wp-content/uploads/2018/01/2017_Celluloid_Ceiling_Report.pdf. Accessed 28 November 2018.

Lebow, Alisa S. (ed.) (2012), *The Cinema of Me: The Self and Subjectivity in First Person Documentary*, London: Wallflower Press.

Lewis, Stephen P., Health, Nancy L., St Denis, Jill M. and Noble, Rick (2011), 'The scope of non-suicidal self-injury on YouTube', *Pediatrics*, 127:3, http://pediatrics.aappublications.org/content/early/2011/02/21/peds.2010-2317?maxtoshow=&hits=10&RESULTFORMAT=&fulltext=YouTube&searchid=1&FIRSTINDEX=0&sortspec=relevance&resourcetype=HWCIT. Accessed 25 October 2017.

Lian, Vigdis (ed.) (2015), *Ta det som en mann, frue!*, Oslo: Emilia Forlag.

Lindi, Marte (2017), 'Når er jeg samisk nok?', NRK, 12 February, https://www.nrk.no/finnmark/xl/nar-er-man-samisk-nok_-1.13364696. Accessed 25 October 2017.

Lindqvist, Ursula (2016), *Roy Andersson's 'Songs from the Second Floor' Contemplating the Art of Existence*, Seattle, WA: University of Washington Press.

Lindøe, Siri H. (2017), 'Den døde gutten på stranden: Etiske og estetiske aspekter ved fremstilling av lidelse i mediene', in C. Hamm, S. H. Lindøe and B. Markussen (eds), *Lidelsens estetikk: sår, sorg og smerte i litteratur, film og medier*, Bergen: Alvheim & Eide Akademisk Forlag, pp. 183–200.

Linga, Steinar J. (2014), 'Humørfylt alvorsfilm. Ingen tabu!', *Helgeland Arbeiderblad*,10 October, p. 6.

LUMIERE Official Website (2018), 'Återträffen (SV)', http://lumiere.obs.coe.int/web/film_info/?id=44460. Accessed 12 June 2018.

Lundberg, Frida (2014), 'The Nordic film industry remains male dominated', *Nordic Information on Gender (NIKK)*, 31 January, http://www.nikk.no/en/news/the-nordic-film-industry-remains-male-dominated/. Accessed 25 October 2017.

Lundby, Ellen-Astri (2017), e-mail to author, 18 September.

——— (2018), e-mail to author, 14 June.

Mackenzie, Catriona (2014), 'The importance of relational autonomy and capabilities for an ethics of vulnerability', in C. Mackenzie, W. Rogers and S. Dodds (eds), *Vulnerability: New Essays in Ethics and Feminist Philosophy*, New York: Oxford University Press, pp. 33–59.

Mackenzie, Catriona, Rogers, Wendy and Dodds, Susan (2014), 'Introduction: What is vulnerability and why does it matter for moral theory', in C. Mackenzie, W. Rogers and S. Dodds (eds), *Vulnerability: New Essays in Ethics and Feminist Philosophy*, New York: Oxford University Press, pp. 1–32.

Mackenzie, Scott and Stenport, Anna W. (2016), 'Contemporary experimental feminist Sami documentary: The first person politics of Liselotte Wajstedt and Elle-Maija Tailfeathers', *Journal of Scandinavian Cinema*, 6:2, pp. 169–82.

Magnusson, Tobias (2016), 'Det är svårt att vara frisk i ett sjukt samhälle', *Sesam*, 28 September, p. 10.

Mann, Sally (1992), *Immediate Family*, New York: Aperture.

Marks, Laura (2000), *The Skin of the Film: Intercultural Cinema, Embodiment, and the Senses*, Durham, NC and London: Duke University Press.

Marsh, Sarah (2017), 'A quarter of young men self-harm to cope with depression, says survey', *The Guardian*, 1 March, https://www.theguardian.com/society/2017/mar/01/quarter-of-young-men-self-harm-cope-depression-poll. Accessed 25 October 2017.

Mattsson, Jonas (2016), 'Jag mådde bättre när kameran var med', *Modern Psykologi*, 2 March, pp. 19.

Mauno, Hanne (2015), 'Fiskerjenten', *Dagsavisen*, 15 August, pp. 22–25.

Migrationsverket (Swedish Migration Agency) (2016), 'Nearly 163,000 people sought asylum in Sweden in 2015', 12 January, https://www.migrationsverket.se/English/About-the-Migration-Agency/News-archive/News-archive-2016/2016-01-12-Nearly-163000-people-sought-asylum-in-Sweden-in-2015.html. Accessed 25 October 2017.

Mikkelsen, Maria and Åsebø, Synnøve (2014), 'Odin ble mobbet på to ulike skoler. Han ble bare 13 år', *VG Spesial*, http://www.vg.no/spesial/2014/odin/. Accessed 25 October 2017.

Minde, Henry (2005), 'Assimilation of the Sami – implementation and consequences', *gáldu čála – Journal of Indigenous Peoples Rights*, 3, pp. 1–33.

The Ministry of Culture, Norway (2006–07), *Veiviseren for det norske filmløftet*, Report 22, https://www.regjeringen.no/no/dokumenter/Stmeld-nr-22-20062007/id460716/. Accessed 25 October 2017.

Mitchell, Wendy (2015), 'Good news for women in film in Norway, Sweden', *Screen Daily*, 19 May, http://www.screendaily.com/festivals/cannes/good-news-for-women-in-film-in-norway-sweden/5088442.article. Accessed 25 October 2017.

Moen, Jørn H. and Husebø-Evensen, Marius (2014), 'Villemo (14) tørket ei tåre da hun så hvor mange som kom i fakkeltog mot mobbing', *Dagbladet*, 16 November, http://www.dagbladet.no/nyheter/villemo-14-torket-ei-tare-da-hun-sa-hvor-mange-som-kom-i-fakkeltoget-mot-mobbing/60872146. Accessed 25 October 2017.

Molloy, Missy, Nielsen, Mimi and Shriver-Rice, Meryl (eds) (2018), *ReFocus: The Films of Susanne Bier*, Edinburgh: Edinburgh University Press.

Montgomery, Hedvig (2016), 'Prisen for det uperfekte', *Rushprint*, 6 April, http://rushprint.no/2016/04/prisen-for-det-uperfekte/. Accessed 25 October 2017.

Nelson, Fraser (2017), 'They won't admit it in Stockholm, but Donald Trump is right about immigration in Sweden', *The Telegraph*, 23 February, http://www.telegraph.co.uk/news/2017/02/23/wont-admit-stockholm-donald-trump-right-immigration-sweden/. Accessed 25 October 2017.

Nermoen, Live (2017), e-mail to author, 8 May.

Ngai, Sianne (2005), *Ugly Feelings*, Cambridge, MA: Harvard University Press.

Nichols, Bill (2010), *Introduction to Documentary*, 2nd ed., Bloomington, IN: Indiana University Press.

Norsk filminstitutt (Norwegian Film Institute) (NFI) (2012), 'Nye veier til lange filmer', 18 January, http://minside.nfi.no/101708/nye-veier-til-lange-filmer. Accessed 4 February 2019.

——— (2014), 'Edith Carlmarprisen til Solveig Melkeraaen', 31 October, http://minside.nfi.no/nyhetsarkiv/edith-carlmarprisen-til-solveig-melkeraaen. Accessed 10 November 2017.

——— (2016), 'Handlingsplan for kjønnsbalanse i film', 29 June, https://www.nfi.no/aktuelt/2016/handlingsplan-for-kjonnsbalanse-i-norsk-film. Accessed 4 February 2019.

——— (2017), *Årsrapport 2016*, https://www.nfi.no/statistikk/statistikk-analyse-og-rapporter. Accessed 25 October 2017.

——— (2018), *Årsrapport 2017*, https://www.nfi.no/statistikk/statistikk-analyse-og-rapporter. Accessed 28 November 2018.

Odell, Anna (2009), *Ukänd, kvinna 2009-349701*, installation, Stockholm: University College of Arts, Crafts and Design.

Olweus, Dan (2001), 'Bullying at school: Tackling the problem', *OECD Observer*, 225, March, http://oecdobserver.org/news/archivestory.php/aid/434/Bullying_at_school:_tackling_the_problem.html. Accessed 25 October 2017.

——— (2010), 'Understanding and researching bullying: Some critical issues', in S. R. Jimerson, S. M. Swearer and D. L. Espelage (eds), *Handbook of Bullying in Schools: An International Perspective*, New York: Routledge, pp. 9–34.

Ording, Oda and Bruland, Severin R. (2017), 'Frykter migrantstrøm av "bibelske dimensjoner"', NRK, 10 July, https://www.nrk.no/urix/frykter-migrantstrom-av-_bibelske-dimensjoner_-1.13596641. Accessed 25 October 2017.

Organization for Economic Co-Operation and Development (OECD) (2009), 'Comparative child well-being across the OECD', *Doing Better for Children*, Paris: OECD Publishing, http://www.oecd.org/els/family/doingbetterforchildren.htm. Accessed 25 October 2017.

——— (2017a), *Health at a Glance 2017: OECD Indicators*, Paris: OECD Publishing, https://www.oecd-ilibrary.org/social-issues-migration-health/health-at-a-glance-2017_health_glance-2017-en. Accessed 22 January 2019.

——— (2017b), *PISA 2015 Results (Volume III): Students' Well-Being*, Paris: OECD Publishing, http://dx.doi.org/10.1787/9789264273856-en. Accessed 25 October 2017.

Orning, Sara (2015), 'Å se film med kroppen', *Wuxia*, 5 October, https://wuxiablog.com/2015/10/05/a-se-film-med-kroppen/. Accessed 25 October 2017.

Orr, Alison and O'Connor, Deborah (2005), 'Dimensions of power: Older women's experiences with electroconvulsive therapy (ECT)', *Journal of Women and Aging*, 17:1&2, pp. 19–36.

Papademetriou, Demetrios G. and Banulescu-Bogdan, Natalia (2016), *Understanding and Addressing Public Anxiety about Immigration (Transatlantic Council Statement)*, Migration Policy Institute, http://www.migrationpolicy.org/research/understanding-and-addressing-public-anxiety-about-immigration. Accessed 26 October 2017.

Pedersen, Helga (2016), 'Er jeg same?', *Nordlys*, 14 November, http://nordnorskdebatt.no/article/same. Accessed 26 October 2017.

Pedersen, Lars H. (2015), ' – Takler ikke nederlag', NRK, 22 January, http://www.nrk.no/ostfold/flest-unge-menn-tar-livet-sitt-1.12163453. Accessed 7 November 2017.

Persen, Bente (2008), '"At bringe dem fram til mands modenhet": En studie av fornorskningen av samene i Porsanger', MA dissertation, Oslo: University of Oslo.

Predelli, Line N., Halsaa, Beatrice, Thun, Cecilie, Perren, Kim and Sandu, Adriana (2012), *Majority-Minority Relations in Contemporary Women's Movements: Strategic Sisterhood*, Basingstoke: Palgrave Macmillan.

Qvortrup, Jens (2009), 'Are children human beings or human becomings? A critical assessment of outcome thinking', *Rivista Internazionale di Scienze Sociali*, 117:3-4, pp. 631–53.

Renov, Michael (2008), 'First-person films: Some theses on self-inscription', in T. Austin and W. de Jong (eds), *Rethinking Documentary: New Perspectives, New Practices*, Maidenhead: Open University Press, pp. 39–50.

Romney, Jonathan (2014), 'The tracking shot: Film-making magic – or stylistic self-indulgence', *The Guardian*, 4 December, https://www.theguardian.com/film/2014/dec/04/tracking-shot-film-making-magic-or-stylistic-self-indulgence-birdman. Accessed 7 November 2017.

Rose, Diana, Fleischmann, Pete, Wykes, Til, Leese, Morven and Bindman, Jonathan (2003), 'Patients' perspectives on electroconvulsive therapy: Systematic review', *British Medical Journal*, 326:7403, pp. 1365–66.

Roxborough, Scott (2016), 'Cannes: U.K. industry targets gender equality in film funding by 2020', *The Hollywood Reporter*, 15 May, http://www.hollywoodreporter.com/news/cannes-uk-industry-targets-gender-894246. Accessed 7 November 2017.

Sauter, Willmar (2012), '*Unknown, woman* by Anna Odell: The event, the trail, the work – Reflections on the mediality of performance', *Theatre Research International*, 37:3, pp. 249–64.

Selby, Hubert Jr ([1978] 1996), *Requiem for a Dream: A Novel*, London: Marion Boyars.

Shields, David (2010), *Reality Hunger: A Manifesto*, London: Hamish Hamilton.

Smedsrud, Morten S. (2015), 'Filmet sønnene i ti år', *Adresseavisen*, 4 February, p. 20.

Socialstyrelsen (The National Board of Health and Welfare) (2016), *Statistics on Pharmaceuticals 2015*, https://www.socialstyrelsen.se/Lists/Artikelkatalog/Attachments/20144/2016-4-25.pdf. Accessed 7 November 2017.

Staksrud, Elisabeth (2013), *Children in the Online World: Risk, Regulation, Rights*, Farnham: Ashgate Publishing.

Statistisk sentralbyrå (Statistics Norway) (SSB) (2018), 'Lønnsforskjellene mellom kvinner og menn fortsetter', 8 March, https://www.ssb.no/arbeid-og-lonn/artikler-og-publikasjoner/lonnsforskjellene-mellom-kvinner-og-menn-fortsetter. Accessed 29 November 2018.

Steinkjer, Mode (2014), 'Personlig balansekunst', *Dagsavisen*, 9 October, p. 33.

Stene, Marianne (2015), 'Jeg kutta meg til blods for å overleve', NRK, 10 October, https://www.nrk.no/dokumentar/xl/_-jeg-kutta-meg-til-blods-for-a-overleve-1.12590444. Accessed 7 November 2017.

Svenska Filminstitutet (Swedish Film Institute) (SFI) (2017a), *Filmåret i siffror: Facts and Figures 2016*, http://www.filminstitutet.se/globalassets/2.-fa-kunskap-om-film/analys-och-statistik/publikationer/filmaret-i-siffror/filmaret-i-siffror-2016.pdf. Accessed 7 November 2017.

——— (2017b), *Goal 2020: Gender Equality in Film Production*, http://www.filminstitutet.se/en/about-us/swedish-film-institute/gender-equality/. Accessed 7 November 2017.

——— (2018), *Filmåret i siffror 2017*, https://www.filminstitutet.se/sv/fa-kunskap-om-film/analys-och-statistik/filmaret-i-siffror/filmaret-i-siffror-2017/. Accessed 29 November 2018.

Sørensen, Britt (2014), 'Realitetsorientering', *Bergens Tidende*, 9 October, p. 44.

Sørensen, Siri Ø. (2014), 'Fortellinger om feminisme og motforestillinger mot statsfeminisme. En analyse av norske avistekster 2007-2011', *Tidsskrift for kjønnsforskning*, 38:3&4, pp. 235–52.

New York Times (2014), 'Combined print & e-book nonfiction', 19 October, https://www.nytimes.com/books/best-sellers/2014/10/19/combined-print-and-e-book-nonfiction/. Accessed 7 November 2017.

Thomassen, Yvonne (2018a), e-mail to author, 15 June.

——— (2018b), e-mail to author, 19 June.

Thomsen, Bodil M. S. (2016), *Lars von Triers fornyelse af filmen 1984-2014: Signal, Pixel, Diagram*, København: Museum Tusculatum.

Tjellaug, Ane B. (2015), 'Sterk selvskadings-selfie', *Vårt Land*, 17 September, pp. 25–26.

Tvedt, Terje (2009), *Utviklingshjelp, utenrikspolitikk og makt: Den norske modellen*, Oslo: Gyldendal akademisk.

Twemlow, Stuart W., Fonagy, Peter and Sacco, Frank C. (2004), 'The role of the bystander in the social architecture of bullying and violence in schools and communities', *Annals of the New York Academy of Sciences*, 1036, pp. 215–32.

UNICEF Child Alert (2017), *A Deadly Journey for Children: The Central Mediterranean Route*, https://www.unicef.org/publications/files/EN_UNICEF_Central_Mediterranean_Migration.pdf. Accessed 7 November 2017.

United Nations (UN) (2016), '244 million international migrants living abroad worldwide, new UN statistics reveal', http://www.un.org/sustainabledevelopment/blog/2016/01/244-million-international-migrants-living-abroad-worldwide-new-un-statistics-reveal/. Accessed 7 November 2017.

United Nations Educational, Scientific and Cultural Organization (UNESCO) (2013), 'Sophus Tromholt Collection', http://www.unesco.org/new/en/communication-and-information/memory-of-the-world/register/full-list-of-registered-heritage/registered-heritage-page-8/sophus-tromholt-collection/. Accessed 7 November 2017.

Urdahl, Mette (2015), 'Mottok filmpris i Edinburgh', *Tvedestrandsposten*, 7 November, p. 13.

Utdanningsdirektoratet (Udir) (2018), 'Elevundersøkelsen 2017: Mobbing og arbeidsro', 22 January, https://www.udir.no/tall-og-forskning/finn-forskning/rapporter/elevundersokelsen-2017-mobbing-og-arbeidsro2/. Accessed 3 December 2018.

van Daalen-Smith, Cheryl L. (2011), 'Waiting for oblivion: Women's experiences with electroshock', *Issues in Mental Health Nursing*, 32:7, pp. 457–72.

White, Patricia (2015), *Women's Cinema, World's Cinema: Projecting Contemporary Feminisms*, Durham, NC: Duke University Press.

Wiell, Maria (2017), 'Att filma var allt som jag kunde då', *Ölandsbladet*, 28 March, p. 13.

Wiking, Meik (2016), *The Little Book of Hygge: The Danish Way to Live Well*, London: Penguin Books.

Witoszek, Nina (2011), *The Origins of the Regime of Goodness: Remapping the Cultural History of Norway*, Oslo: Universitetsforlaget.

World Health Organization (WHO) (2017), 'Depression', http://www.who.int/mediacentre/factsheets/fs369/en/. Accessed 7 November 2017.

Østbø, Stein (2016), 'Sophie Elise doblet inntekten i 2015', VG, 13 October, http://www.vg.no/rampelys/sophie-elise/sophie-elise-doblet-inntekten-i-2015/a/23819823/. Accessed 7 November 2017.

Åsebø, Synnøve, Mikkelsen, Maria and Olsen, Geir (2014), 'Arrangerer fakkeltog mot mobbing etter Odin-saken', VG, 11 November, http://www.vg.no/nyheter/innenriks/mobbing/arrangerer-fakkeltog-mot-mobbing-etter-odin-saken/a/23333941/. Accessed 7 November 2017.

Filmography

Films marked with an asterisk have not been cited in the book, but they are part of my corpus and have informed my readings, hence I have mentioned them in the filmography list.

Aronofsky, Darren (2000), *Requiem for a Dream,* USA: Artisan Entertainment.

*Bashi, Ahang (2009), *Paradiset* (*The Paradise*), Sweden: Dramatiska Institutet, Stockholm.

——— (2016), *Skörheten* (*Fragility*), Sweden: Momento Film.

Bendjelloul, Malik (2012), *Searching for Sugar Man*, Sweden, UK and Finland: Red Box Films, Passion Pictures, Canfield Pictures (in association with).

*Bergsmark, Ester M. (2012), *Pojktanten* (*She Male Snails*), Sweden and Denmark: Upfront Films.

Big Brother (2001–03, 2005–06, Norway: TVNorge).

——— (2011, Norway: TV2 Bliss).

——— (2014, Norway: FEM).

Bigelow, Kathryn (2008), *The Hurt Locker,* USA: Voltage Pictures, Grosvenor Park Media (in association with), Film Capital Europe Funds (FCEF) (in association with).

*Bjemar, Magnus and Kærn, Simone A. (2006), *Smiling at a War Zone*, Denmark: Cosmo Film, Hepp Film, Klaffi Productions.

*Blickfeldt, Emilie (2013), *How Do You Like My Hair?*, Norway: Nordland kunst- og filmfagskole.

Block, Doug (2005), *51 Birch Street*, USA: Copacetic Pictures, HBO/Cinemax Documentary, ZDF Enterprises, Priddy Brothers Entertainment.

——— (2009), *The Kids Grow Up*, USA: Copacetic Pictures, Hard Working Movies (in association with), ZDF/Arte.

*Brask, Dorte H. (2002), *Min elskede* ('My darling'), Denmark: Easy Film.

Bron/Broen (*The Bridge*) (2011–18, Sweden and Denmark: Filmlance International AB, Nimbus Film Productions, Sveriges Television SVT).

Campion, Jane (1993), *The Piano,* New Zealand, Australia and France: CiBy 2000, Jan Chapman Productions, The Australian Film Commission (with the assistance of), New South Wales Film & Television Office (with the assistance of).

Demme, Jonathan (1991), *The Silence of the Lambs*, USA: Strong Heart/Demme Production, Orion Pictures.

Don't Call Me Crazy (2013, UK: BBC).

*Engberg, Mia (2013), *Belleville Baby*, Sweden: Story AB, Sveriges Television (SVT).

Farmen (2001, Norway: TV2).

Forman, Miloš (1975), *One Flew over the Cuckoo's Nest,* USA: Fantasy Films.

Generation Jihad (2010, UK: BBC).

Girls (2012–17, USA: HBO).

*Halle, Mariken (2011), *Kanske i morgon* ('Maybe tomorrow'), Sweden: Filmhögskolan i Göteborg.

Hammer, Anders S. (2017), *Ranias flukt* ('Rania's escape'), Norway: Norsk Rikskringkasting (NRK).

Haneke, Michael (2012), *Amour*, Austria, France and Germany: Les Films Du Losange, X-Filme Creative Pool, Wega Film.

Hanssen, August B. (2014), *Idas dagbok* (*Ida's Diary*), Norway: Chezville, Indie Film as, Mouka Fili Oy, Nordisk Film SchortCut, Substans Film, Telling Productions, Topscore music (music composition).

*Haq, Iram (2009), *Skylappjenta* (*Little Miss Eyeflap*), Norway: SF Norge A/S, Storm Films.

*——— (2013), *Jeg er din* (*I Am Yours*), Norway: Mer Film.

*——— (2017), *Hva vil folk si* (*What Will People Say*), Norway, Germany and Sweden: Mer Film, Rohfilm Factory GmbH, Zentropa International Sweden.

*Haugsgjerd, Anne (1986), *Livet på Frogner* (*Life in Frogner*), Norway: Anne Haugsgjerd.

*——— (1991), *Flink pike, sitt pent!* (*Good Girl...Sit Down!*), Norway: Anne Haugsgjerd.

*——— (2014), *Opp Ned er Alt Abstrakt...sa pappa* (*Upside Down Everything is Abstract...My Father Said),* Norway: Anne Haugsgjerd.

*Hoel, Anniken (2017), *Dødsårsak: Ukjent* (*Cause of Death: Unknown*), Norway: ManifestoFilm.

Holm, Aslaug (2006), *Oljeberget* ('The rich country'), Norway: Fenris Film.

——— (2015), *Brødre* (*Brothers*), Norway: Fenris Film.

Iñárritu, Alejandro González (2014), *Birdman or (The Unexpected Virtue of Ignorance),* USA: New Regency Pictures, M Productions, Grisbi Productions.

Jackson, Peter (2001), *The Lord of the Rings: The Fellowship of the Ring*, New Zealand and USA: New Line Cinema, WingNut Films, The Saul Zaentz Company.

——— (2002), *The Lord of the Rings: The Two Towers,* New Zealand and USA: New Line Cinema, WingNut Films, The Saul Zaentz Company.

——— (2003), *The Lord of the Rings: The Return of the King,* New Zealand and USA: New Line Cinema, WingNut Films, The Saul Zaentz Company.

Jensen, Knut E. (2001), *Heftig og begeistret* (*Cool and Crazy*), Norway: BarentsFilm AS, Giraff Film AB, Norsk Film.

Kernell, Amanda (2016), *Sameblod* (*Sami Blood*), Sweden, Norway and Denmark: Bautafilm, Det Danske Filminstitut, Digipilot.

*Kramvig, Britt and Andersen, Rachel G. (2014), *Dreamland,* Norway: Sonarfilm.

Linklater, Richard (2014), *Boyhood*, USA: IFC Productions, Detour Filmproduction.

Lucas, George (1977), *Star Wars,* USA: Lucasfilm, Twentieth Century Fox.

Lundby, Ellen-Astri (2009), *Min mors hemmelighet* (*Suddenly Sami*), Norway: Ellen Lundby film&media, Sonarfilm DA.

*——— (2014), *Joikefeber* (*Yoik Fever*), Norway: Ellen Lundby film&media.

Melkeraaen, Solveig (2006), *Begavede barn* ('Talented children'), Norway: Exposed Filmproductions AS, TV2.

——— (2008), *Statistikk* ('Statistics'), Norway: Speranza Film A/S.

——— (2009), *Fabelaktige Fiff og Fam* ('The fabulous Fiff and Fam') Norway: Speranza Film AS v/Thomas Robsahm.

——— (2014), *Flink pike* (*Good Girl*), Norway: Medieoperatørene AS v/Ingvil Giske.

Mikhalkov, Nikita (1994), *Anna ot 6 do 18* (*Anna: 6-18*), Russia: Caméra One, Trite Productions.

*Myren, Hanne (2013), *Elsk meg* ('Love me'), Norway: Motlys.

*Nango, Marja B. (2011), *Halvt ditt, halvt datt* (*Half of This, Half of That*), Norway: Nordland kunst- og filmfagskole.

Nordaas, Aleksander (2012), *Thale*, Norway: Film Fund FUZZ, Yesbox Productions.

Odell, Anna (2013), *Återträffen* (*The Reunion*), Sweden: French Quarter Film.

*Olin, Margreth (2003), *Kroppen min* (*My Body*), Norway: Speranza Films A/S.

——— (2012), *De andre* (*The Others*), Norway: Speranza Films A/S.

*——— (2016), *Mannen fra Snåsa* (*Doing Good*), Norway: Speranza Films A/S.

*Orvung, Benedicte M. (2010), *Strengt hemmelig* ('Top secret'), Norway: Orvung Film.

Pedersen, Janus M. (2010), *Armadillo*, Denmark: Fridthjof Film.

*Pichler, Gabriela (2012), *Äta sova dö* (*Eat Sleep Die*), Sweden: Anagram, Film i Väst, Solid Entertainment.

Pontecorvo, Gillo (1960), *Kapò*, Italy, France and Yugoslavia: Cineriz, Vides Cinematografica, Zebra Films.

Prager, Wilhelm (1931), *Eine reise unter der Mitternachtssonne* ('A journey under the midnight sun'), Germany: Universum-Film AG (UFA).

*Randhav, Begonia (2016), *Stödgruppen (The Support Group)*, Sweden: Retina Randhav Film.

Renais, Alain (1959), *Hiroshima mon Amour*, France and Japan: Argos Films, Como Films, Daiei Studios.

Ridley, Scott (2001), *Hannibal*, USA and UK: Metro-Goldwyn-Mayer (MGM), Universal Pictures, Dino De Laurentiis.

Scorsese, Martin (1990), *Goodfellas*, USA: Warner Bros.

*Steinhoff, Linda (2015), *Voldtatt* (*Raped*), Norway: ITV Studios Norway.

*Straume, Unni (2014), *remake.me*, Norway: USF International.

*Tailfeathers, Elle-Máijá (2014), *Bihttoš* (*Rebel*), Canada and Norway: Elle-Máijá Tailfeathers and Laura Good.

Tailfeathers, Elle-Máijá and Nango, Marja B. (2012), *Colonial Gaze Sami Artists' Collective (Skabmagovat),* Norway: Elle-Máijá Tailfeathers and Marja Bål Nango.

Thomassen, Yvonne (2013), *Familiebildet* (*My Family Portrait*), Norway: Alligator Film A/S.

Vinterberg, Thomas (2012), *Jagten* (*The Hunt*), Denmark and Sweden: Danmarks Radio (DR), Det Danske Filminstitutet, Eurimages.

*Västrik, Linda (2000), *Pappa och jag* ('Dad and me'), Sweden.

*Wajstedt, Liselotte (2007), *Sami nieida jojk* (*Sami Daugther Yoik*), Sweden: Filmpool Nord, Little Big Productions.

Welles, Orson (1958), *Touch of Evil*, USA: Universal International Pictures.

Östlund, Ruben (2014), *Turist* (*Force Majeure*), Sweden, France, Norway and Denmark: Beofilm, Coproduction Office, Motlys.

——— (2017), *The Square,* Sweden, Germany, France and Denmark: Plattform Produktion, Arte France Cinéma, Coproduction Office.

Øvredal, André (2010), *Trolljegeren* (*Trollhunter*), Norway: Filmkameratene A/S, Film Fund FUZZ, SF Norge A/S.

Index